IMAGES OF THE PAST
WEMBLEY STADIUM

IMAGES OF THE PAST

WEMBLEY STADIUM

The History of the Iconic Twin Towers

MAURICE CROW

PEN & SWORD HISTORY

First published in Great Britain in 2018 by
PEN & SWORD HISTORY
an imprint of
Pen & Sword Books Ltd,
47 Church Street,
Barnsley,
South Yorkshire
S70 2AS

A CIP record for this book is available from the British Library.

ISBN 978 1 52670 207 4

Typeset in Gill Sans 11/13 by
Aura Technology and Software Services, India
Printed and bound in India by Replika Press Pvt. Ltd.

Pen & Sword Books Limited incorporates the imprints of Atlas,
Archaeology, Aviation, Discovery, Family History, Fiction, History, Maritime,
Military, Military Classics, Politics, Select, Transport, True Crime, Air World,
Frontline Publishing, Leo Cooper, Remember When, Seaforth Publishing,
The Praetorian Press, Wharncliffe Local History, Wharncliffe Transport,
Wharncliffe True Crime and White Owl.

For a complete list of Pen & Sword titles please contact
Pen & Sword Books Limited
47 Church Street, Barnsley, South Yorkshire S70 2AS, England

E-mail: enquiries@pen-and-sword.co.uk
Website: www.pen-and-sword.co.uk

Contents

Additional research by Juliet Morris, George Letheren Smith and Yves Brown.

Introduction

It was the field of dreams, the birthplace of legends, the hallowed home of our sporting gods. Historic Wembley Stadium, with its iconic Twin Towers, was truly the most revered of venues.

Until 2002–2003, when the world-renowned colossus was demolished to make way for its futuristic replacement, the famous old Stadium witnessed some of the most heroic events of the twentieth century. But its history, although always exciting, was also often uncertain – and not a little bizarre.

So, despite most eyes being on future fixtures as the sporting hub heads towards its centenary, it is the old edifice's often forgotten past that is the subject of this book.

The uncomfortable truth is that Wembley's original debut was anything but auspicious. In fact, it was once viewed as a debt-ridden disaster.

So doomed was the North London complex deemed to be once it had fulfilled its original purpose that it was about to be knocked down – rescued, only at the last moment, in the most extraordinary circumstances. Happily, it recovered to become a success story, and the memories recorded here will hopefully open the floodgates of nostalgia for followers of sport.

Wembley, it must be remembered, came to the rescue of the first post-war Olympics when no other nation on earth would accept the challenge. It gripped greyhound racing aficionados and it resonated with the roar of the followers of speedway stars. The giants of American football also muscled in to display their skills there. Great British boxing champions like Frank Bruno and Henry Cooper stepped into the ring and Cassius Clay was felled to the canvas before stunned fans. And, of course, Wembley crowds gasped in awe at the footwork of Stanley Matthews and wept in ecstasy at the triumph of Bobby Moore.

But Wembley is more than just the holy grail of sporting venues. It has seen defining moments in pop music history, such as Live Aid. It has given platforms to the Pope and evangelist Billy Graham. It has staged breathtaking spectacles no other venue could hope to accommodate, growing in stature over the course of an astonishing century.

This, then, for both sports buffs and social historians, is historic Wembley's story – an unfolding saga played out beneath those symbolically soaring Twin Towers.

Wembley Stadium

Extraordinary as it may now seem, Wembley was not built as a sporting stadium. It was the result of an ambitious scheme to glorify the British Empire with an exposition of literally groundbreaking scale and ingenuity. Its chosen location in North West London was already the home of one folly – a strange, half-built structure – but would soon be criticised as the site of another. For the original Wembley project of a century ago was, in its early years, mocked as a disastrously ruinous fool's paradise.

The Wembley story begins not long after the First World War when the government of King George V came up with a project to celebrate the rich diversity of the Empire with a majestic showcase. The leafy site chosen was the home of a half-built tower known as Watkin's Folly, the result of an ill-conceived attempt to create a rival attraction to the Eiffel Tower in Paris. Sadly for its creator, Sir Edward Watkin, the new tower's concrete foundations shifted when the structure reached 200 feet and the project was abandoned.

The surrounding area was a picture of semi-rural bliss, with green fields to which Londoners flocked for picnics and days out 'in the country'. Not much had changed since the earliest recorded history of the area, when the Saxon King Offa valued Wembley at thirty shillings – a mere £1.50. In AD 757, he knew the place as Wemba's Clearing, or Wemba's Lea.

The Lodge, Wembley Park.

Above and previous page: scenes of peaceful, rural, leafy Wembley ... soon to be transformed by steel and concrete into the most famous sporting venue on the planet.

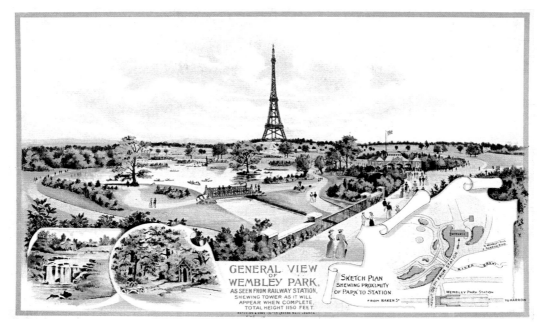

GENERAL VIEW OF WEMBLEY PARK, AS SEEN FROM RAILWAY STATION, SHEWING TOWER AS IT WILL APPEAR WHEN COMPLETE. TOTAL HEIGHT 1150 FEET.

SKETCH PLAN SHEWING PROXIMITY OF PARK TO STATION. FROM BAKER ST.

An over-optimistic impression of a future Wembley Park surmounted by Watkin's Folly.

Above left: Watkin's Folly under construction ... although this was as far as the ambitious project ever got.

Above right: Abandoned and under demolition: the ignominious end of Sir Edward Watkin's dream to create a rival to the Eiffel Tower.

Right: With Watkin's Folly removed and the ground levelled, foundations are laid for the Stadium.

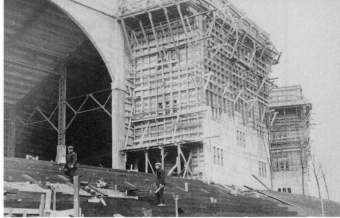

'Bigger than Rome's Coliseum' was the boast as 25,000 tons of concrete formed the new Stadium.

However, when plans for the new Empire Stadium, designed by Sir Owen Williams, were agreed in 1922, change was swift, dramatic and irrevocable. Watkin's Folly was demolished and 250,000 tons of soil and clay were removed to level the site. In just 300 days, the magnificent edifice that was to become the most famous stadium in the world rose from the rubble. The creation swallowed 25,000 tons of concrete, 2,000 tons of steel and half a million rivets, and was completed at a cost of just £750,000. Legend had it that a train was somehow buried underneath the Stadium during construction but the mystery, which lingered for more than seventy-five years, was solved only when work on a new Wembley Stadium began in 1999 … and not even a wagon wheel was found.

Back in 1923, the site engineers realised they needed to test the strength and durability of their magnificent new creation, so they enlisted an entire battalion of infantry and hundreds of building workers to march around the new terraces. Naturally their structure proved to be sound and solid.

The great boast was that the Stadium was 'bigger than the Coliseum in Rome', at 890 feet long (271 metres), 650 feet wide (198 metres) and 126 feet (38 metres) to the top of the trademark Twin Towers. The walls, they said, were as high as the Wall of Jericho – and it wouldn't be long before they were under siege!

*   *   *   *   *

Everything was ready for a spectacular opening, which is exactly what the Empire Stadium got. Although it was built to house the great Empire Exhibition of 1924, the Stadium was completed in time to host the 1923 FA Cup Final. Fundraising for the project had been helped by a stirring speech from Edward, Prince of Wales and, more prophetically, the Football Association's interest in staging its future Cup Finals there. FA Cup Finals had previously been played at Kennington Oval, at Crystal Palace and, from 1920 to 1922, at Stamford Bridge, Chelsea.

When the great day – 28 April 1923 – dawned, players of Bolton Wanderers and West Ham United arrived at Wembley for the biggest, most spectacular, most memorable Cup Final of them all. But it was a sporting 'first' that almost became a farcical 'last', not so much memorable for the game itself but for the fact that most of England seemed to try to squeeze into the new Stadium to watch the battle for the biggest prize in British soccer.

Above right: Colourful cover of the first Cup Final programme.

Below: On the day of its first Cup Final, a human tide flooded to Wembley.

An estimated 250,000 fans headed towards Wembley on 28 April 1923.

Many fans who failed to get through the turnstiles clambered over the walls.

The ground's estimated capacity was 120,000 but, as no one expected quite so many to turn up on the day, a decision was made to allow payment at the turnstiles for those without tickets. The official attendance was 126,047, and that number was already inside the Stadium soon after one o'clock. However, when the gates were shut at 1.45 pm, the surrounding area was still a heaving mass of fans, all heading for the game. They swarmed over railings, turnstiles and crash barriers by the hundred, climbed drainpipes, scaled walls and generally burrowed their way inside the Stadium by any means they could. Those already inside the ground spilled over onto the pitch in their thousands.

When King George V arrived at 2.45 pm, barely a blade of grass could be seen for the milling throng. No one could see them but somewhere in the midst of the human sea, the massed bands of the Brigade of Guards could be faintly heard playing *God Save the King*. Police attempts to restore order were proving futile – until the appearance of Constable George Albert Scorey mounted on a magnificent pale horse called Billy. In what has become known as the 'miracle of the white horse', PC Scorey and his 13-year-old mount somehow managed to part the crowd and gently coax them back behind the touchlines.

The valiant policeman later recalled:

> As my horse picked his way onto the field I could see nothing but a sea of heads and thought it was impossible to clear it. But I told myself not to be beaten and chanced to see an opening near one of the goals. The horse was very good, easing them back with his nose and his tail until we got the crowds back along one of the goal lines.

Those fans along the touchline joined hands and, with Billy parading in front of them, heaved backwards, step by step, until the pitch was cleared. The game started forty minutes late, and although the attendance cannot be confirmed, it is thought about 250,000 were watching.

A mass of excited humanity surrounds the Royal Box (*above*) and flows onto the pitch in anticipation of the kick-off for Wembley's first Cup Final.

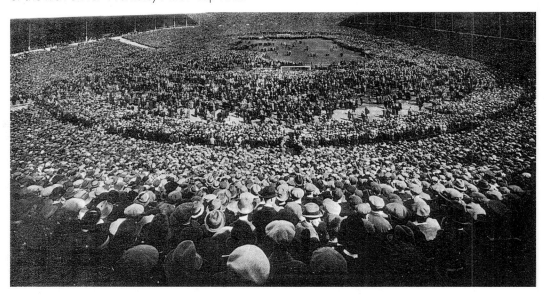

Within two minutes of the kick-off, Bolton took the lead as David Jack scored Wembley's first-ever goal, which came as a West Ham player was still trying to climb back out of the crowd next to the touchline! Ted Vizard, the Bolton left-winger, found no space at all down the touchlines but hotly denied that the best pass he received all day was from a spectator. George Kay, the West Ham captain, tumbled into the crowd and before he could get back

Police attempts to restore order at first proved futile as fans meandered across the pitch.

Mounted police were out in force but it was Constable George Scorey, on a white horse called Billy, who finally coaxed the 1923 Cup Final crowd off the pitch.

A gentlemanly sport: the captains of Bolton and West Ham shake hands before the kick-off.

onto the pitch he heard a terrific roar. Bolton had scored again, and Kay didn't see it. Neither did Jack, who plunged into the crowd as he whipped over a cross from the byline. Bolton's centre forward, Joe Smith, smashed the ball home but it came back so quickly from the net that the goal was disputed. It was thought by some to have bounced off the posts but actually rebounded from the spectators pressed against the back of the net. Referee David Asson confirmed the score and Bolton held on to their lead for the first Wembley FA Cup Final win.

It was a bitter-sweet result for Bolton's visiting dignitaries; such was the chaos that the directors, travelling separately from the team, did not see a single ball kicked! And it wasn't a great commercial success for the FA either, as they had to refund 10 per cent of the gate money to the 50,000-plus who could not get to their places.

The story of the 'White Horse Final' made headlines all around the world – something Wembley has been doing ever since.

*   *   *   *   *

The next event in Wembley's calendar was the long-planned celebration of the nation's imperial influence: the great British Empire Exhibition of 1924. But even as preparations for this were being made, soccer matches still went ahead. In January, the FA held special matches with several clubs (including Arsenal, Chelsea and Wolves) who had blank Saturdays after being knocked out of the FA Cup. The result of their experiment: the two-man offside plan

Artists' impressions of some of the attractions of the British Empire Exhibition of 1924.

was adopted in time for the 1925–26 season. In April, the England team played their first Wembley game. The 1–1 draw with Scotland was almost lost amidst the frantic preparations for the great exhibition. And only a few days after the opening ceremony, Wembley staged its second FA Cup Final when Newcastle United beat Aston Villa 2–0. Newcastle's victory is less remembered than the club's £750 fine imposed by the Football League for allegedly fielding deliberately weak teams in the seven games leading up to the final.

But even soccer's dramas were overshadowed by Wembley's hosting of what, at a cost of £12 million, was the largest and most expensive exhibition ever staged anywhere in the world. Its officially stated aim was to:

> stimulate trade, strengthen bonds that bind Mother Country to her Sister States and Daughters, to bring into closer contact the one with each other, to enable all who owe allegiance to the British flag to meet on common ground and learn to know each other.

The great British Empire Exhibition was opened by King George V and Queen Mary, appropriately on St George's Day, 23 April, with the monarch's first-ever radio broadcast to his subjects. His declaration was flashed around the world and eighty seconds later it was delivered back to the King by a messenger boy in the form of a telegram. The splendid royal procession heralded two years of colourful celebrations, which attracted 27 million visitors, each paying the equivalent of 7½ pence admittance.

Although the Empire Stadium was the first building completed, it was one of four gigantic edifices housing the exhibition, plus an extensive amusement park of Disneyland proportions, complete with rollercoaster, water chute and scenic railway. The site covered 219 acres and was so vast that a non-stop railway ran around it. There were 'palaces' of Industry, Engineering and Art, while the Stadium housed a popular Empire Pageant, Boy Scouts Jamboree and an enormous Imperial Choir, which took up half the Stadium. One of the greatest of those

A plaster horse arrives to join the pageantry as the final decor is added to the exhibition.

King George V and Queen Mary arrive by carriage for the opening ceremony on 23 April.

Crowds welcome the King and Queen at the exhibition on, appropriately, St George's Day.

An alternative form of transport for ordinary visitors was by boat on a newly created lake.

THE LAKE

Aerial photograph of Wembley Stadium with some of the exhibition pavilions in the foreground.

The Australian Pavilion was one of the major attractions that, in total, covered 219 acres.

early thrills was the International Rodeo, presented by showman Charles B. Cochran, who brought cowboys and cowgirls from across the Atlantic, along with 400 head of cattle and 400 horses. The crowds loved the displays of trick riding, bronco busting and steer roping. Of the fifty-eight territories that composed the Empire at the time, fifty-six participated with displays and pavilions, the only exceptions being tiny Gibraltar and Gambia.

By Direction of the LIQUIDATORS.

The Right Honourable J. H. THOMAS, M.P.   Sir JAMES A. COOPER, K.B.E.
Sir ARTHUR WHINNEY, K.B.E.

WEMBLEY

Within Eleven minutes by Electric Railway of the West End.

Illustrated Particulars, Plans & Conditions of Sale

OF THE

FREEHOLD

OF THE

British Empire Exhibition

EXTENDING TO

136 acres.   2 roods.   39 poles.

Approached by two Railways and the Principal Arterial
Roads in the West of London.

The Property contains numerous Permanent Buildings

INCLUDING

THE PALACE OF ENGINEERING.   THE PALACE OF INDUSTRY.
THE PALACE OF ARTS.   THE CIVIC HALL.
NUMBER OF RESTAURANTS.   ADMINISTRATIVE BUILDINGS.

AND

THE STADIUM.

Extensive areas of

VALUABLE BUILDING LAND

supplied with all public services and many miles of hard core roadway

To be offered for Sale by Auction as a whole, by Messrs.

KNIGHT, FRANK & RUTLEY

(Sir Howard Frank, Bart., G.B.E., K.C.B., F.S.I.; Alfred J. Burrows, F.S.I.; Arthur Horace Knight, F.A.I.)

In the Estate Sale Room, 20, HANOVER SQUARE, LONDON, W.1.
On   1926.

Solicitors:—Messrs. SLAUGHTER & MAY, 18, Austin Friars, E.C. 2.
Auctioneers' Offices:—20, HANOVER SQUARE, LONDON, W. 1.; 90, Princes Street, Edinburgh;
78, St. Vincent Street, Glasgow; 41, Bank Street, Ashford, Kent.
Telephone:—MAYFAIR 3066 and 314.

The original document announcing the auction sale of Wembley in 1926.

In 1925, massive crowds continued to flock to the British Empire Exhibition but the Stadium remained a sporting venue throughout, with a terrific turnout to see Cardiff City become the first Welsh team in an FA Cup Final. Sheffield United, however, sank Welsh hearts and hopes with the only goal of the game. Football of a different code made its first Wembley appearance that year when the Army met the Royal Air Force in a game of Rugby Union. Wembley didn't have another Rugby Union game until 1942.

Bolton Wanderers lifted their second FA Cup at Wembley in 1926, beating Manchester City 1–0 thanks again to David Jack. City suffered the double disaster of losing not only the final but being relegated from the First Division in the same season.

In 1927, Cardiff City returned to dent London's pride by beating Arsenal 1–0. The hymn Abide With Me was introduced for the first time at this final and has been a key feature of the big match build-up ever since. The tradition was the suggestion of Fred Rinder, who was connected with Aston Villa, and song sheets were subsequently handed out to the crowds at almost every final for the next four decades.

Ingloriously, in November 1925, the British Empire Exhibition Association had been voluntarily wound up and the buildings, including the Stadium, were to be auctioned off. Incredibly, although 90,000 people an hour had visited the exhibition at its peak, the whole event made a spectacular loss. With total costs for the exhibition put at £12 million, something like £10 million had to be found by those who had underwritten the event.

Stock Exchange speculator James White thought he had pulled off the deal of the century when he snapped up the Wembley complex for £300,000. However, the site was described by other commentators at the time as 'a vast white elephant' and a 'rotting sepulchre of hopes and the grave of fortunes'. The only bright note for Wembley was the promise from the Football Association that they would stage two games a year there. White was undeterred and set about making a profit by selling off the various parts of the great Wembley site.

Enter Arthur J. Elvin. A cigarette kiosk attendant during the exhibition, he was the son of a Norwich policeman and had served in the RAF during the First World War, ending up a prisoner of war after his Bristol biplane was forced down. Returning home penniless, a £4 10s-a-week job as kiosk attendant was found for him by the Ex-Officer's Association. But by the end of the British Empire Exhibition he owned eight kiosks and had branched out into souvenirs and confectionery.

Elvin asked for and was given one of the exhibits, the 'Lifeboat House', which he broke up and sold. He went on to buy, demolish and sell other buildings. The Palestine Building became a Glasgow laundry, the West African building a furniture factory and the East African building a jam factory. Some buildings became part of Bournemouth and Boscombe Football Club's grandstand. Eventually, Elvin negotiated the purchase of the Stadium itself for £122,500, agreeing to pay the money over ten years.

Soon afterwards, however, site owner James White shot himself and Elvin was forced to find the money within a matter of days. At 6.30 pm on 17 August 1927, Arthur Elvin became owner of the Empire Stadium. At 6.31 pm he sold it for £150,000 and took his profit in shares. The new owners were the Wembley Stadium and Greyhound Racecourse Company, soon to become Wembley Stadium Ltd, with Arthur Elvin as managing director.

*   *   *   *   *

It was yet another astonishing twist in Wembley's fate and fortunes. Only a couple of years earlier the demolition men had been waiting. And that is how the story of Wembley might have ended: as another expensive folly. Instead the lowliest in the land arrived to rescue this symbol of shattered imperial pride … as Wembley Stadium went to the dogs. And like a greyhound after catching sight of the hare, it never looked back.

From the moment the first traps sprung open on 10 December 1927, Greyhound Racing was a vital factor in making the Stadium pay, a fact recognised years later by the then general manager, George Stanton, who said: 'For the best part of fifty years, the greyhounds were the Stadium's bread and butter. Soccer and the like were the jam, but without the dogs I doubt if we would have survived.'

As a sport, greyhound racing was in its infancy, having been introduced to Britain only in 1926. An investment of more than £90,000 had been required to make the necessary changes to track, kennels and lighting, but the first greyhound meeting attracted a crowd of 50,000 and attendances during the first year exceeded 1,500,000. Under the stewardship of Captain Arthur Brice, Wembley quickly gained a reputation for high

Kiosk owner Arthur Elvin snapped up the Empire Stadium in 1927 – and relaunched it as Wembley Stadium Ltd.

standards, fair racing and quality entertainment. In 1928, it hosted the first meeting of the National Greyhound Racing Society, from which the National Greyhound Racing Club developed. It was quickly dubbed 'the Ascot of Greyhound Racing', regularly pulling in up to 10,000 paying customers each meeting to watch what was at that time said to be Britain's biggest spectator sport.

The most famous greyhound of them all, Mick the Miller, entered sporting folklore as a Wembley hero in the early 1930s. Although born in Ireland, he is celebrated as the

first great racing greyhound to compete in England. By the end of his short three-year racing career, marked by his final race at Wembley in 1931, he had become a worldwide icon in the sport. His achievements include winning nineteen races in a row, including the English Greyhound Derby on two successive occasions. Mick the Miller was not only the star of the track but also of the silver screen: in 1933, accompanied by his owner, Mrs A.H. Kempton, he appeared in the title role of the 1934 comedy film *Wild Boy*.

Half a century elapsed before any rival emerged to equal Mick the Miller's celebrity. Ballyregan Bob and Scurlogue Champ were four-legged favourites in the mid-1980s. Ballyregan Bob set a world record for thirty-two straight wins and Scurlogue Champ won fifty-one out of sixty-three races, and set no less than eighteen track records. In 1985, Wembley paired them in what was billed as the 'Ultimate Match'. Sadly, Scurlogue Champ broke down after two bends, leaving Ballyregan Bob to beat the rest by 12 lengths – the only time the two legends ever met.

*   *   *   *   *

Greyhounds had saved Wembley Stadium during the 1920s, its financially darkest days when the country was still impoverished in the aftermath of the First World War. But the dogs weren't the only attraction to draw the crowds. The longest journey to North West London was probably the road from Scotland, along which in 1928 the 'Auld Enemy' invaded – their fans even bringing along scaling ladders to get into the ground. They dished out such a lesson

Mick the Miller was a hero of the thirties, winning nineteen consecutive races. He was also a celebrated movie star, taking title role in the film *Wild Boy*.

to England that they became known as 'the Wembley Wizards' and their 5–1 victory was no more than they deserved on the day.

In the FA Cup, Blackburn Rovers scored three goals to Huddersfield Town's single goal, in the first final to be broadcast on BBC Radio. It meant that for the first time fans at home could hear the emotive chant *Abide With Me* as the highlight of the community singing, led by Thomas P. Ratcliff, dressed all in white.

The following year, Bolton secured their third FA Cup victory in seven years by beating Portsmouth 2–0. But other sports made 1929 especially memorable …

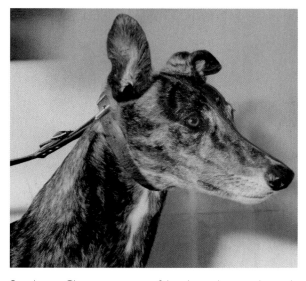

Scurlogue Champ was one of the champion greyhounds that rescued Wembley's fortune in the twenties.

Rugby League, previously a strictly northern affair, arrived in May when the first Challenge Cup Final was played at Wembley. A crowd of 41,500 gathered to watch Wigan beat Dewsbury 13–2. Admission prices started at just two shillings (10p) for standing, with reserved seats from five shillings (25p).

The crowd sing *Abide With Me* at the 1928 Cup Final between Blackburn and Huddersfield.

Gate receipts were £5,614, with each team receiving £350 – barely enough for a post-match round of drinks these days. Dewsbury were no match for Wigan, a super-strong team blessed with players like Jim Sullivan, Lou Brown, Tom Parker and Roy Muir Kinnear (father of comedian/actor Roy Kinnear and grandfather of actor Rory Kinnear).

Most importantly, the 1929 match launched a fabulous new sporting tradition that helped make Wembley Stadium the southern home of this traditionally 'northern' sport. As Rugby League's oldest and most prestigious competition, it is the only knockout tournament of its kind as teams from the community game, university and the services all compete alongside professional Rugby League clubs. Apart from 1932, when Wembley was unavailable, and during the Stadium's rebuilding, the title has continued to be contested there ever since.

*   *   *   *   *

The other sport that roared into Wembley in 1929 was two-wheeled. Speedway, which had arrived in Britain from Australia as 'dirt track racing', had already begun to catch on. Keen to embrace the new sport, Wembley created a cinder track inside the greyhound track and a 'Wembley Lions' team was formed.

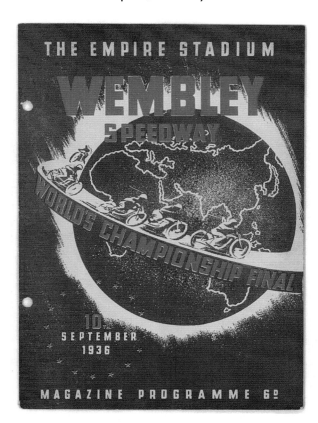

Wembley became the regular venue for the Speedway World Championship.

However, poor performances from the Lions – they lost nine of their first eleven League matches – were reflected in poor attendances: less than 3,000 fans isolated in the 100,000-plus capacity venue.

The turnaround came when Lions team manager Johnnie Hoskins scoured the country for new talent, which in turn justified Arthur Elvin in promoting the Wembley Speedway Supporters Club. By the end of their inaugural season, the membership (at two shillings, or 10p, each) soared to 20,000 and meetings drew up to 40,000 fans.

Hoskins, who was a born showman, added extra attractions to pull in the crowds. Track staff marched into the Stadium to the tune *Entry of the Gladiators* and stunt shows and circus acts filled the intervals. One of the showmen, known as Professor Powsey, specialised in setting himself on fire and diving into a 4-foot deep tank.

Waiting for the 'off' ... From the thirties onwards, Wembley became the speedway capital of the world.

Welshman Freddie Williams (*left*) was one of Britain's brightest speedway stars, winning the World Final twice as a Wembley Lion.

Others crashed motorcycles through plate glass. Stunt ace Putt Mossman was famed for his hair-raising spectaculars.

Top names of the day who thrilled the crowds on the amazing Wembley track included Australians Vic Huxley, Lionel Van Praag and Jack Young, Americans Jack and Cordy Milne, and England's Roger Frogley, Jack Parker, Bill Kitchen and Peter Craven. In the early thirties, Australian Bill Lamont gained cult status. He was nicknamed the 'Man with a Month to Live' because of his death-defying track craft. Riding flat-out, only seeming a hair's breadth from the fence, he was also called the 'Programme Snatcher' by enthralled fans because he could, quite easily, have stretched out a hand and taken a programme from the crowd.

After their faltering start back in 1929, the Wembley Lions gave their fans plenty to roar about, picking up three League Championships by 1932 and the National Trophy for the second year in succession. In 1936, Wembley became the annual venue for the World Final. The Wembley Lions were the sport's dominant team, winning the League Championship ten times in eighteen seasons. Before the end of the decade, a world record crowd of 85,000 turned out to see American Jack Milne become speedway's world champion.

*   *   *   *   *

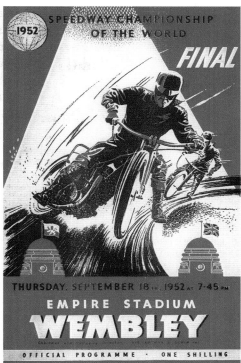

Stars like Alf Bottoms (*left*) helped maintain speedway's popularity at Wembley well into the fifties.

Meanwhile, throughout the thirties it was soccer that continued to make the headlines. During that decade, Wembley was firmly established as the home of the England team. It also felt, at times, like the second home of Arsenal, because manager Herbert Chapman's Gunners were there three times for Cup Finals.

In 1930, Arsenal beat Huddersfield 2–0 but the game is best remembered for the incredible sight of the German airship, the *Graf Zeppelin*, sailing quietly over the Stadium. Seven years later, the newsreels recorded a horrific reminder of that flypast when its massive sister ship, the *Hindenburg*, burst into flames on landing in the US, with the loss of thirty-three lives. Meanwhile, back in 1930, England played Germany at football – motorcycle football – with speedway favourite Colin Watson as England centre forward. And in the traditional game, England gained revenge on the Scots for their hammering of two years previous, with a 5–2 victory.

It was the turn of the Midlands to enthral and entertain in 1931 when West Bromwich Albion beat Birmingham 2–1, the first Wembley victory for a Second Division club. Albion also achieved a memorable double by gaining promotion.

Arsenal were back in 1932 to face Newcastle United in the Cup but they lost in controversial circumstances. Having taken the lead, Arsenal defenders forced Newcastle winger Jimmy Boyd away from the danger area as he dribbled towards the dead ball line. They stopped as Boyd carried the ball out of play, but he crossed it into the penalty area and Allen put Newcastle back on terms. Uproar followed but the referee never saw the

A silent but dramatic visitor from Germany: the *Graf Zeppelin* flies over Wembley in 1930.

A gyroscope hovers over a crowded Stadium – though the more orthodox form of transport to Wembley for millions of fans was the train.

King George V presents the FA Cup to Tom Parker, the Arsenal captain, in 1930. On the far left is the future King George VI.

In 1933, the Cup Final teams' shirts were numbered for the first time – from one to twenty-two!

ball cross the line. The goal stood and Allen added the winner for Newcastle eighteen minutes from time. Arsenal fans still refer to this as the Cup they were 'cheated out of'.

Rugby League fans also, perhaps, felt a little cheated in 1932. After three successful Wembley Challenge Cup finals, the competition returned to the north as Wigan played host to the final between Leeds and Swinton. The crowd was less than half the size of the previous Wembley crowds and an important lesson was harshly learned: that Wembley adds a sense of occasion.

Teams wearing numbers on their shirts have been a familiar part of the game for decades but in 1933 it was a novelty. Everton played Manchester City in a Lancashire derby, with players wearing numbers for the first time – not, as you might imagine, each

Aerial photograph shows the Stadium crowded for the 1933 Cup Final between Everton and Manchester City.

team going up to eleven, but numbered from one to twenty-two. This was the heyday of Dixie Dean, who scored the middle goal in Everton's 3–0 win.

City were back to make amends the following year, when Fred Tilson scored both goals as they ended Portsmouth's Cup dream with a 2–1 win. The referee was Stanley Rous, later Sir Stanley, in whose name the annual England–Scotland fixture would be fought. Another memorable name on the pitch that day was Manchester City's right half-back, the young Matt Busby.

A degree of pomp and pageantry returned as the newly built Wembley Arena helped host the British Empire Games of 1934 along with the White City – with the Stadium assuming a supporting role for once, providing the venue for a flag-waving ceremonial and a soccer tournament.

Wembley and White City shared the Empire Games in 1934.

Police escort, thirties style ... Sheffield Wednesday captain Ronnie Starling is carried from the pitch shoulder high in 1935.

There was another 'first' for Wembley in 1934, when baseball was played at the Stadium. The crew of the heavy cruiser USS *New Orleans* were keen to stage a game and they appealed to the American Ambassador for help. Wembley obliged, and on 16 June, the ship's A and B teams slugged it out at the by now world famous venue.

With the opening of the Empire Pool and Sports Arena – soon to be known simply as Wembley Arena – next door to the Stadium in 1934, many other sports were able to share in the thrill of appearing 'at Wembley', albeit without the big occasion atmosphere of the Stadium itself.

Boxing was one such sport, with British and Commonwealth heavyweight champion Jack Petersen savouring the unique experience of both the Stadium and the Arena. Four months after taking a battering from German giant Walter Neusel at the Arena, Petersen took him on again, this time in front of 50,000 cheering fans at the Stadium in 1935. Rain didn't dampen the crowd's enthusiasm as Petersen looked to be gaining the upper hand. With Neusel distressed and reeling in the ninth round, Petersen walked into a desperate left thrown by the German, which opened up his old eye wound. Though he continued to fight like a hero, the Welshman couldn't press home his advantage after that, and Neusel

King George VI and Queen Elizabeth congratulate Sunderland captain Raich Carter on lifting the 1937 FA Cup.

A sea of flat caps, trilbies and bowlers are addressed by loudhailer.

Wild enthusiasm ... Whether these Wembley fans are running towards or away from the Stadium is not recorded.

went home the victor once again. The outbreak of a rather more serious punch-up between Britain and Germany meant there would be no more boxing at Wembley until after the war.

Meanwhile, West Brom returned to the Stadium for the 1935 Cup Final, losing 4–2 to Sheffield Wednesday. It was the other steel town side, Sheffield United, who took on Arsenal in 1936. This time, the Yorkshire men went down 1–0 to an Arsenal side that fielded six England internationals, including goal scorer Ted Drake.

The Cup Final of 1937 between Sunderland and Preston North End was memorable for more than the Wearsiders' 3–1 victory. In a dispute that would not be amiss today, the newsreel companies had fallen out over rights to film the match. In the end, Wembley made their own arrangements to film the game, resulting in an added attraction for the crowd. Hired planes and autogyros (early helicopters) buzzed the ground throughout as the frantic newsreel companies battled to get pictures of the game. In one sense, the game was quite literally 'on Sky'.

At the opposite end of the sporting spectrum, probably the most genteel event ever held at Wembley Stadium also took place in 1937, when 6,000 members of the Women's League of Health and Beauty exercised to music for the Coronation Pageant. Prunella Stack led the ladies, who were experts in the 'Bagot-Stack Stretch and Swing System'. Whoever thought aerobics was a modern invention?

Less elegant were the FA Cup visitors from Preston, who were back in 1938 to produce the first Wembley final to go into extra time. The dying seconds were ticking away when Huddersfield defender Alf Young tripped Preston's George Mutch. A spot kick was awarded and Mutch tucked it away, even though time had officially expired. It was the first time many people realised that the rules allow for a penalty awarded before the final whistle to be taken after it should have officially been blown.

Darker days were just around the corner as Wolverhampton Wanderers headed for the Twin Towers, hot favourites to beat Portsmouth in the 1939 FA Cup Final. Rumour abounded that Wolves had secret scientific training and amazing 'wonder treatment' glandular injections. However, they were destroyed by Pompey's old-fashioned use of two quick wingers and the Midlanders slumped to a 4–1 defeat. On a Cup trivia note, Pompey then held the FA Cup for a longer period than any other team. It was, of course, not competed for during the Second World War, which broke out later that year.

*　　*　　*　　*　　*

By the end of August 1939, the lights of Wembley were extinguished and the Stadium was plunged into a virtual five-year blackout throughout the Second World War. The World Speedway Championships, due to take place in September, were cancelled and on the first day of war, 200 greyhounds were evacuated from the Wembley kennels to a country farm. Within a short period, however, limited greyhound racing, during the afternoon, was allowed to return to the Stadium. With little sport to cheer about, the BBC broadcast dog racing for the first time at the 1940 Spring Cup. Commentator Raymond Glendenning crammed more words into the half-minute race broadcast than anyone believed possible as a dog called Junior Classic beat Majestic Sandhills by a neck.

It was not long before Wembley was called upon to do 'its bit' for the war effort. After the evacuation of Dunkirk, the Stadium and Arena were turned into emergency dispersal centres as thousands upon thousands of weary troops were brought home. As the troops left, weekly greyhound meetings continued, along with the occasional football match – home internationals and wartime Cup Finals.

Wales had made their first appearance at Wembley against England on 13 April 1940, winning by the only goal of a game, scored by Arsenal's Bryn Jones. The crowd was limited to 40,000 to make for easy dispersal in the event of an air raid.

Eight weeks later, Blackburn Rovers met West Ham United in the first Football League War Cup Final. Despite the fears that London would be bombed, fans came roaring in to watch the game at Wembley, itself an obvious Luftwaffe target. A thirty-fifth-minute goal from the Hammers' outside right, Sam Small, was enough to clinch the Cup for the East Londoners.

After that match, West Ham and Blackburn players received gold medals but all contestants in subsequent wartime finals received National Savings Certificates as their mementoes of the game. And in the case of wartime internationals, no caps were awarded to players who took part. Instead, they received an illuminated address from the Football Association, listing all the games in which they had played from 1939 to 1946.

Those wartime events were memorable for the ingenuity in staging them at all. With the country concentrating on the war effort, most major competitions had to be abandoned. Hundreds of footballers having signed up to fight – including, for example, ninety-one from Wolves and sixty-plus each from Huddersfield, Leicester and Charlton – England's best teams were depleted. Because of this, many clubs fielded 'guest' players instead.

A 60,000 crowd saw Arsenal and Preston North End fight out a one–all draw in the 1941 War Cup Final with a young Denis Compton netting the equaliser for Arsenal. Preston went on to win the replay 2–1 at Ewood Park, Blackburn. In October, Winston

Churchill was in the crowd that saw England beat Scotland 2–0, with goals from Don Welsh and Jimmy Hagan. It wasn't his first wartime visit to Wembley. The year before, Winston had attended an Arena ice gala, at which his Wembley hosts joked that it was 'the only time Winnie got cold feet'!

After 1941, the country's 50-mile travel ban meant that Cup Finals were split between north and south. Other wartime games were also clouded by the absence of players serving their country, but the 1942 Amateur Cup Final was able to boast more professional players than any other 'amateur' game ever played. Wealdstone beat RAF Uxbridge 4–1 despite the RAF side lining up an impressive list of servicemen who, before the war, played for league clubs. The RAF side included Corporal Clack (Brentford), Corporal Forder (Crystal Palace), Leading Aircraftman Dale (Portsmouth), Corporal McGregor (Manchester City), Sergeant Vause (Rochdale), Leading Aircraftman Johnson (Newcastle United) and Corporal Mullinger (Aston Villa). And still they lost.

Men in uniform were a familiar sight at every event but there was most definitely an unusual look to the 'uniforms' of the two teams who met one Saturday in September 1943. Men from the US Air Force took on the US Ground Forces in a traditional baseball match – and every player on the park was a professional back home in the States. The crowd was heavily laden with American servicemen but the British section were helped in following the game thanks to a specially erected scoreboard and an explanatory commentary. They were nevertheless just as bemused as any American would have been trying to follow a game of cricket!

With the tide of the war turning after the Normandy D-Day landings on 6 June 1944, it looked as though Wembley would escape physically unscathed. Then, early one morning in August 1944, a flying bomb – known to Londoners as a 'doodlebug' – dropped from the skies. It landed some 50 yards from the greyhound kennels, although only two of the 150 dogs inside at the time were hurt. The others scampered off in all directions and it was more than a week before all were safely rounded up.

Wembley helped to keep morale flying as high as the flags fluttering from the Twin Towers during the war by maintaining the great sporting traditions and by hosting parties, presentations and jamborees for military and civilians. And for the soldiers, sailors and airmen serving in foreign fields, Wembley and all it represented shone like a beacon.

Five soldiers serving in the Burma jungles wrote to Wembley bosses in 1945 to say:

> As we sit here in the jungle we are thinking of dear old Wembley and the 1945 Cup Final. For the past fourteen months we have been fighting the Jap with the magnificent 14th Army and I can assure you that amusements have been very limited. But football has been played whenever possible.

The five soldiers had been on leave in April that year and had managed to watch Chelsea beat Millwall 2–0 in the Southern Cup. Also among the spectators were three kings: King George VI, King Haakon of Norway and King Peter of Yugoslavia. There had been a bit of a problem when both teams turned up at Wembley with blue shirts. A set of white

England shirts were quickly found and the Millwall badges were taken off their blue shirts and hastily sewn over the top of the England badges for the match.

When Germany surrendered early in May 1945, a Wembley thanksgiving service was scheduled. On Sunday, 13 May, Thomas P. Ratcliff returned in his white suit to conduct the community singing, backed by a 500-strong choir and a crowd almost too great for the grand Stadium to hold. Wembley's big heart was, perhaps, reflected in the fact that £140,000 had been raised there for the Red Cross and other war charities – a fabulous amount during especially harsh times.

A 'Victory International' between England and France was played out to an honourable 2–2 draw on 26 May, and eight months later, England played their last 'unofficial' international of the war years, beating Belgium 2–0. A young Billy Wright made his first of many appearances for England.

A joyful 1945 'Victory International'.

*   *   *   *   *

In many walks of life, peacetime presented a new, sometimes daunting, challenge after the grim years of war. Wembley was again at the forefront, ready to satisfy a huge thirst for entertainment from a public that had been starved of it for six years. A record number of 4,400,000 spectators attended events there during 1946.

Roaring back into action came the Wembley Lions Speedway stars, lifting the 1946 National League championship, the first of seven titles in eight years. On 13 June 1946, the day that Arthur Elvin was awarded a knighthood, he saw a record crowd of 72,000 witness the Lions beat Birmingham. That summer, the sport pulled in a staggering 1,211,355 supporters for twenty-two fixtures, a weekly average of 55,000-plus. By 1948, the Supporters Club was 61,000 strong, the biggest in the world. Speedway at Wembley was at its peak of popularity.

Rugby League returned, too, with a thrilling final between Wigan and Wakefield Trinity. Wigan led 12–11 when, seconds from time, Wakefield were awarded a penalty. Their skipper, Billy Stott, placed the ball for the last kick of the match – and watched delighted as it soared between the posts for the winning points. With thrills like that, it's no wonder that by 1949

Above and below: The 1947 Final, which saw Charlton take the Cup, marked the first appearance of Wembley legend Arthur Caiger, known as the 'Man in the White Suit', who conducted pre-match community singing.

the Rugby League Challenge Cup Final drew a capacity 95,000 crowd for the first time. (In 1946, Wakefield's Billy Stott became the first winner of the Lance Todd Trophy, awarded in memory of the former Wigan player and Salford manager who died in a road accident on the way home from a game at Oldham.)

The FA Cup restarted in 1946 with a first visit from Derby County, their glorious Cup run thanks largely to inside forwards Raich Carter and Peter Doherty. After ninety minutes they were level with Charlton Athletic 1–1. But in extra time two goals from Jack Stamps and one by Doherty clinched a 4–1 County victory.

In 1947, Charlton returned to claim the Cup with a 1–0 win over

Burnley, who had outplayed the Londoners for most of the game. That event saw the first appearance of a Wembley legend: a character known universally as the 'Man in the White Suit'. He was Arthur Caiger DCM, a former First World War hero and later a London headmaster, who took over the important role of conducting pre-match community singing at the Charlton–Burnley final and continued the tradition until his retirement in 1962. With more than 80,000 voices belting out *Abide With Me* every year, one couldn't really call him an 'unsung hero' but he was certainly a bit of a mystery figure to the millions who tuned into Cup Final coverage around the world. Having rehearsed the Royal Marines band a few days earlier, Caiger would don his white suit and climb to the rostrum as the Stadium began to fill, and would keep the crowds singing until the teams emerged shortly before three o'clock. He would pick songs suitable for both sets of supporters, such as *Loch Lomond* for Scotland, *Land of My Fathers* for Wales and *Ilkley Moor Baht 'At* for a Yorkshire team. *Abide With Me* was always the final tune.

A less tuneful sound caused the most mysterious sporting debacle of 1947, during an April match in which England drew with Scotland 1–1. With twelve minutes remaining, England's Raich Carter looked certain to score after receiving a great ball from Tommy Lawton. With only the keeper to beat, he hesitated, looked at the ref, and fluffed his shot, hitting it straight at Miller, the Scots' goalie. Afterwards he revealed that he definitely heard a whistle blow. 'I knew I was onside but I checked instinctively,' he said. He couldn't make out if the referee was waving him to play on or giving offside, and when he eventually recovered, the chance was gone. Many fans still believe a mystery Scottish whistle-blower in the crowd cost England victory that day.

Above and overleaf: The Road to Wembley ... Post-war Britain saw a boom in car traffic – at which poorer fans could only stand and stare.

Neutral observers of the 1948 Cup Final wanted to see Stanley Matthews pick up a winner's medal as his Blackpool side took on mighty Manchester United. Although Blackpool led 2–1 at half-time, they were denied by a tremendous United performance, which saw the Cup heading for Manchester after a 4–2 win. Stan's fans would have to wait until 1953 before Matthews climbed the steps to receive a winner's award.

The tradition of the Rugby League Cup Final was also now well established at Wembley. And in the late forties, another tradition – seen at every major soccer game today – was introduced by rugby's then administrator, Bill Fallowfield. He introduced the individual presentation of players to the guest of honour before a match. 'It was very much against the wishes of Arthur Elvin at the time,' he once recalled. 'But when he saw it in action he was the first to congratulate me.' The practice was particularly memorable at the 1948 final played at Wembley on 1 May, when a crowd of almost 100,000 saw Wigan beat Bradford 8–3. This was also the first televised Rugby League match and the first ever attended by the reigning monarch, King George VI, who presented the trophy.

*   *   *   *   *

George VI was soon back at Wembley for a more auspicious occasion – one that had the entire world applauding. On 29 July, the King opened the Games of the XIV Olympiad. The first post-war Olympics were a triumph of every kind. A celebration of peace and a symbol of how sport could reunite a world torn apart by conflict, the 1948 summer Games could not have taken place anywhere else. No one else could have made the necessary arrangements in less than two years to host the globe's biggest sporting event. Wembley did – and, from the darkest days of modern history, lit the flame that rescued the Games.

How it happened is a story that is epic even by modern standards. Europe had been ravaged by war. Cities were still in ruins. Across the rest of the globe, nations were struggling out of the abyss to which the years of conflict, cruelty and genocide had condemned them. The last Games had, notoriously, been held in Berlin in 1936, when the Olympic ideal had been corrupted and turned into a propaganda exercise by the Nazi regime. After that, two Olympic years – 1940 and 1944 – had been wiped from the sporting calendar by the Second World War. London had been due to host the latter event, which is why the capital was now offered the Games of the XIV Olympiad for 1948.

But surely it was an impossibility? London was on its knees. Could the one rich, surviving nation not rescue the Games? The United States had considered bidding to stage the Games – until it was recognised that it would be virtually impossible for the impoverished European nations to travel across the Atlantic at such a critical time. After that, it quickly became clear that no one else was willing to make the undertaking to host such a monumental event. So Britain bravely agreed.

It would be the second occasion that London had hosted the Olympics, the city previously being the venue in 1908. At that time, the capital had been at the height of Imperial power, hope and glory. Forties Britain was a very different land, still in the grip

Wembley to the rescue ... Preparing the Stadium for the 1948 Olympic Games.

of wartime rationing, with food, fuel and building materials in desperately short supply. London, blitzed and battered for five years, had ended up broke and with more bomb sites than usable sporting venues. One iconic stadium had survived, however: Wembley. And it was in the shadows of the Twin Towers that the major events of what became known as 'the Austerity Games' were to be held.

After the VE and VJ Day celebrations had died down and sombre reality had set in, there remained only two years to meet the deadline of restoring the Games to their regular schedule. In 1946, Sir Arthur Elvin, who was knighted that year for his services to sport, rose to the challenge of creating a modern facility suitable for the post-war period. Firstly, to cope with the crowds, a new road was created from a specially enlarged Wembley Park Tube station to the Stadium. It was called Olympic Way, although sports fans have always known it as Wembley Way. The Wembley local authorities realised that hosting the Olympics would have to be non-profit making, but still offered to bear the £120,000 cost of creating the new route and infrastructure. For work inside the Stadium itself, a special Act of Parliament was required to make structural changes, build modern dressing rooms, recondition the terraces, widen corridors and improve car parking facilities.

At pitch level, substantial reconstruction was also required. The running track, first laid down in 1923, had long been buried beneath the greyhound course, so with only three weeks to go before the opening ceremony, 100 workmen began the awesome task of recreating a world-class running surface. They dug down to the foundations, laid 800 tons of specially prepared cinders and used the latest scientific measuring equipment to set the

The Australian Olympic team arrive in procession at Wembley Stadium.

The Olympic torch lit a flame for peace across Europe from Greece to England.

levels and distances. The excellence of their work in creating that brand-new track resulted in seventeen world and Olympic records being broken during the course of the Games.

Because of food shortages and rationing, it was agreed that Britain should not bear full responsibility for feeding the athletes. So the visiting teams actually arrived with their own supplies! Any surplus food was then donated to local hospitals. Athletes were allowed to break rationing rules, being given increased rations to match the intake of British dockers and miners – 5,467 calories a day as opposed to the normal 2,600 calories.

Housing the contestants was also hand-to-mouth. No Olympic village was erected, the athletes instead being accommodated in schools, military camps and private homes. The bulk of the male athletes were housed at RAF and Army camps and the women in dormitories at women's colleges.

Some sporting events, such as gymnastics and rowing, were earmarked for other sites far beyond Wembley, of course, but the eyes of the world were on the Stadium when the Games officially opened on 29 July, with teams from fifty-nine nations comprising more than 4,000 competitors (3,714 men, 390 women). Wembley itself would see thirty-three track and field events being contested by more than 800 athletes from fifty-three of those countries. Significant absentees were Germany and Japan, the aggressors of the

Cambridge University quarter-miler John Mark carries the torch on its final leg.

Second World War, who were not invited to participate. Significant entrants included competitors from countries now ruled by Communist governments.

An impressively vast timber scoreboard had been constructed and a concrete platform laid to house the Olympic Flame. On a brilliantly sunny opening day, King George VI, Queen Elizabeth, Queen Mary, Princess Margaret, the Duke and Duchess of Gloucester, the Duchess of Kent, and Lord and Lady Mountbatten – plus 85,000 commoners – watched an impressive ceremony, serenaded by the massed bands of the Brigade of Guards. Seven thousand pigeons, symbolising doves of peace, were released and a 21-gun salute was followed by the arrival of the Olympic Flame, borne aloft by Cambridge Blue John Mark.

The welcome speech to the athletes was given by the Games chairman, Lord Burghley, president of the Amateur Athletics Association and a gold medal winner at the 1928 Olympics. He set the tone by urging them to 'keen but friendly rivalry'. London, he said, represented 'a warm flame of hope for a better understanding in the world which has burned so low'.

He added this rallying call:

> Your Majesty, the hour has struck. A visionary dream has today become a glorious reality. At the end of the worldwide struggle in 1945, many institutions and associations were found to have withered and only the strongest had survived. How, many wondered, had the great Olympic Movement prospered?

The answer might well have already been provided by Baron Pierre de Coubertin, founder of the International Olympic Committee. These were the first Games to be held following his death in 1937, but his noble sentiments were particularly pertinent in a Europe so recently ravaged by war: 'The important thing in the Olympic Games is not winning but taking part. The essential thing in life is not conquering but fighting well.' And so it proved.

The torch beneath the Olympic motto.

Many names unknown to the British public became overnight heroes. One of the most renowned figures to emerge at the 1948 Games was Emil Zátopek, then an unknown Czech army officer, who smashed the world 10,000 metres record by twelve seconds. He also finished second behind Gaston Reiff of Belgium during a driving rainstorm in the 5,000 metres. Zátopek, nicknamed the 'Czech Locomotive', went on to dominate distance running for years to come. He topped his Wembley performance by winning three gold medals at the 1952 Helsinki Olympics: gold in the 5,000 and 10,000 metres, plus a bonus gold when he decided at the last minute to compete in the first marathon of his life.

Back at Wembley, drama surrounded the end of the 1948 marathon as the first man to enter the Stadium, Belgium's Etienne Gailly, stumbled into view exhausted and almost unable to run. As the crowds willed him on, Argentina's Delfo Cabrera and Britain's Tom Richards passed him, with Cabrera winning the gold, Richards the silver and Gailly struggling across the line to take the bronze.

The decathlon provided an equal surprise. It was won by Bob Mathias of the United States – at the age of just seventeen. He became the youngest ever Olympic gold medallist in athletics, an even more remarkable achievement given that he had only taken up the event earlier that year at the instigation of his high school coach. When asked how he would celebrate, the Californian teenager replied: 'I'll start shaving, I guess.' Mathias went on to win all eleven decathlons he contested over the next twelve years, including the retention of his title at Helsinki in 1952.

Another kind of breakthrough in London came in the high jump when America's Alice Coachman became the first black woman to win an Olympic gold medal in track and field with a leap of 1.68 metres. Coachman had dominated this discipline since 1939 but had been unable to demonstrate her Olympic supremacy because of the war. In 1948,

John Mark has the honour of lighting the Olympic Flame in front of King George VI.

she made her winning jump (then marked as 5 ft 6⅛ in) on her first try. Her unlucky rival, Great Britain's Dorothy Tyler, matched it, but only on her second try.

A pioneer of Caribbean athletics, Arthur Wint became the first Jamaican to win an Olympic gold medal. Wint had come to Britain during the war and served as a flying officer in the RAF. He went on to study as a doctor and ran simply for enjoyment, appearing at London's White City stadium to excite the crowds with his 440 yards and 880 yards dashes. But it was at Wembley that he made his mark internationally. He took the silver medal behind America's Mal Whitfield in the 800 metres, then went on to win the 400 metres ahead of his more fancied Jamaican teammate Herb McKenley, with Whitfield third. His 46.2 seconds equalled the Olympic record. Sadly, the 28-year-old 'Gentle Giant', as he was nicknamed, missed his third medal in the London Games by pulling a muscle in the 4 x 400 metres relay final. Tragedy struck when, seized by cramp, Wint collapsed on the cinder track and his team did not finish. Heroic Dr Wint later returned to the city of his greatest sporting triumph when he became Jamaican High Commissioner to London from 1974 to 1978.

Another competitor of professional distinction was Frenchwoman Micheline Ostermeyer, a highly talented concert pianist whose delicate hands proved versatile at

Gaston Rieff of Belgium after narrowly defeating Emil Zátopek of Czechoslovakia in the 5,000 metres. A few days earlier, Zátopek (*below*) had lowered the 10,000 metres word record by twelve seconds.

Legendary heroine of the 1948 Olympics, Fanny Blankers-Koen receives her gold medal for the 200 metres. Silver went to Britain's Audrey Williamson and bronze to America's Audrey Patterson.

Wembley. The 25-year-old, who graduated from the Conservatoire de Paris with high honours, had spent the war at her family's home in Tunis, where she was the star of a classical radio show. But Wembley Stadium saw her most celebrated performance, winning gold medals in both the shot put and discus – despite having picked up a discus for the first time just a few weeks before the event. She also took the bronze at the high jump.

After winning the shot put, Ostermeyer ended the day by performing a Beethoven concert for fellow team members at their headquarters. While continuing her career as a pianist, she went on to win twelve French titles. As such a talented all-rounder, she would have been a prime candidate for the pentathlon but the multi-event competition was not added to the Olympic programme until many years later.

Ostermeyer's performance was only overshadowed by that of one other woman in 1948. She was the legendary Dutch woman Fanny Blankers-Koen, who won four gold medals – and could well have won six if she had been encouraged to compete in two other events. The next occasion any woman came close to matching her feat was in 1988, when the American Florence Griffith Joyner raced to three golds and a silver in Seoul. Twelve years earlier, the Dutch teenager had appeared at the Berlin Olympics, where she had finished sixth in the high jump. While there, she had asked Jesse Owens for an autograph. Now, in London, Blankers-Koen matched her hero's achievement. But it had not been an easy path to glory.

Blankers-Koen already held the world record for the 100 yards when Germany invaded Holland in 1940. Suffering under Nazi occupation, she continued to train and compete

King George VI salutes the athletes, recorded by the fledgling BBC Television service.

Unveiling of the commemoration tablets listing the 1948 Olympic champions.

Close-up of one of the pair of commemoration tablets, which is still housed at the new Wembley Stadium.

when opportunity allowed but by the time of the London Games in 1948, there was little indication that this unassuming mother of two would become the heroine of the 'Austerity Games'.

Yet Blankers-Koen, the 'Flying Dutchwoman', won gold medals in the 100 metres, 200 metres, 80 metres hurdles (in which she set a new world record) and 4 x 100 metres relay – four of the only nine events that women could enter at that time. If she had also contested the long jump and high jump, she could well have won those as well, because they were both disciplines in which she was the current world record holder. As it transpired, the long jump winning mark was far short of her personal best. Incredibly, however, her chances had been dismissed beforehand by Jack Crump, the secretary of the Amateur Athletics Association, who suggested that, at thirty and with two children, she was too old to enter.

After the Games, Blankers-Koen arrived home to a rapturous welcome. In sharp contrast to the riches that subsequent Olympians have earned, Holland's heroine was rewarded by the city of Amsterdam with a new bicycle. The 'Flying Dutchwoman', who died in 2004 at the age of eighty-five, never asked for nor expected anything more.

Interviewed at the age of eighty, she said:

> With the war so soon over, we were surprised but happy that Britain was organising an Olympic Games but I had no great expectations of it – nor of myself, because I had had two babies during the war.
>
> I remember the Wembley track had been made only weeks before the event. It was cinder and there had been quite a lot of rain but we were just very happy to be able to run and compete again. There was no Olympic village and we girls were housed in a school, six to a room, about half an hour's journey by train from the Stadium. We used to walk to the station, wait for a train and then make our own way to Wembley. Now athletes are very well looked after. It is a great commercial business enterprise these days. Back then there was much more in the way of friendship and we were all happy just to be taking part.

Football played its natural part, with a fiercely contested Olympic soccer tournament. Great Britain lost in the semi-finals to Yugoslavia but the eventual winners were Sweden. Britain were runners-up in the hockey, losing to India in the final. There were also six equestrian events held at the Stadium. The gold medal places were dominated by French, Mexican, Swiss and American riders. Indeed, overall, Great Britain did not rank high in the medal tables, trailing in twelfth place in a list topped by the United States, Sweden and France. But it didn't seem to dent national pride. The bigger boast was that Wembley had won a worldwide reputation.

By the time the London Olympics closed on 14 August, total expenditure on the 'Austerity Games' had amounted to just £600,000, and final accounts showed profits of £10,000. They sound small sums by today's standards but they reflected a different age and different tastes and values. The era of professionalism, or even semi-professionalism, had not yet dawned and the events at Wembley and beyond were conducted in the most innocent and honest sporting spirit. American broadcaster Siegmund Smith summed up the spirit of the day with these words: 'I record my genuine admiration for the achievements of the British people, not only in staging the Games but in staging them the way they did. I liked the crowd's behaviour at every event and I admired their sportsmanship.'

The Games of the XIV Olympiad had been a triumph in every way: a celebration of peace and a symbol of how sport could unite a war-weary world. What had seemed an impossibly daunting challenge at a time of post-war hardships was hailed around the globe as an ultimate triumph. It was an achievement that lifted the pride of ration book Britons and made Wembley Stadium a name instantly recognised as the most famous sports venue in the world.

*   *   *   *   *

The dramatic decade of the 1940s drew to a close with English soccer's latest sensation, young Billy Wright, making his first Wembley Cup Final appearance. In 1949, Wright helped Wolverhampton Wanderers to an impressive 3–1 win over fancied Leicester City. His two previous appearances on the lush green turf had been with England against Scotland.

Into the 1950s, and a golden era for football fans as Stanley Matthews and Tom Finney, Jackie Milburn, Nat Lofthouse and the great 'Busby Babes' team of Manchester United all graced the glorious game with their presence at Wembley. But there was tragedy lurking, too, and the myth of England's invincibility at home was also due to be shattered.

Arsenal, captained by Joe Mercer, started the decade as Cup winners. Two goals from Reg Lewis gave them victory over Liverpool in the first final to enjoy a new 100,000 capacity attendance.

The once-in-a-lifetime thrill of appearing at Wembley was also offered for the first time to England's schoolboys as the Schools' FA were allowed to stage matches there. And for fans of American football, 1950 saw this great game arrive at Wembley. The first game took place in December when the Fürstenfeldbruck Eagles from

Princess Elizabeth hands the FA Cup to Wolves captain Billy Wright in 1949.

the USAF's West German base took on Burtonwood in the USAF Europe Championships. The Eagles won 27–6.

A year later, 30,000 spectators cheered on the English and Irish teams in the first All-England Women's Hockey Association encounter. England won 6–1. The awesome noise of thousands of schoolgirls screaming, cheering, blowing whistles, ringing bells and waving rattles created a cacophony that became known as the 'Wembley Whistle'. It created problems for players and umpires, and eventually a scientific study was carried out to find a way of letting the umpires be heard on the pitch. A report to the Hockey Association concluded: 'The noise at its maximum was of such volume that no whistle blown by human lungs could be heard against it.' Attendances climbed steadily and the ladies shrugged off the 'St Trinian's Day' tag awarded to the regular support of some 60,000 highly vocal schoolgirls, to add yet another fine sporting spectacle to Wembley's rich tapestry of talents.

In soccer, it was Newcastle United's Milburn who earned distinction in 1951, scoring in every round before delivering the two goals that sank Blackpool in the final. The Geordies were back to lift the Cup again in 1952 (the first team to win it back-to-back since 1891) with a 1–0 win over Arsenal. In an era when foreign players were few and

In 1952, it was Prime Minister Winston Churchill's turn to meet FA Cup winners Newcastle United.

Newcastle captain Joe Harvey is raised aloft by team mates after receiving the FA Cup from Winston Churchill.

far between, it was Newcastle's Chilean player George Robledo who headed the only goal five minutes from time.

Home internationals against Wales and Northern Ireland were played on Wembley's turf for the first time in the 1950s. The Welsh got their first taste of Wembley in a 5–2 defeat in 1952 whilst the Irish went down 3–0 in 1955. The great Jimmy McIlroy helped Northern Ireland to wreak their revenge in 1957, scoring alongside Sammy McCrory and Bill Simpson to give Northern Ireland a 3–2 win.

*   *   *   *   *

In 1953, following the death a year earlier of King George VI, a joyful Coronation created a new Queen, Elizabeth II … and Wembley created a new king of soccer, Stanley Matthews. In that year's FA Cup Final, it looked for all the world as though Blackpool's 'Wizard of Dribble' was to be denied a winner's medal for the third time in six years. With only twenty minutes left, his team were 3–1 down to a solid looking Bolton Wanderers. With breathtaking skill, Matthews proceeded to turn Bolton's defence inside out, delivering pinpoint crosses for his fellow forwards. Stan Mortensen converted one cross from Matthews before adding an equaliser with a thundering free kick. As extra time loomed, Matthews again took the ball to the byline and delivered a perfect centre for Bill Perry to score the winner. George Farm, goalkeeper for Blackpool in that memorable encounter, said: 'It was a one-man show and the understanding that Stanley had with the rest of the forward line was quite unbelievable.'

Even though Stan Mortensen notched the first hat-trick scored at Wembley, the game became known as 'the Matthews Final'. It reinforced Sir Stan's reputation as the supreme master of the sport. He is also celebrated throughout the game as one of its most gentlemanly players.

Matthews, who grew up in the Potteries supporting Port Vale, honed his legendary skills and finely tuned balance by arranging chairs in a line in his back garden and constantly dribbling around them. He joined Stoke City as a 17-year-old apprentice, moving on to Blackpool

Stanley Matthews, the legendary 'Wizard of Dribble', steers the ball past a Bolton opponent to clinch the 1953 Cup Final for Blackpool.

Royal fans greet the 'king of the pitch' ... King George VI shakes the hand of Stanley Matthews before the 1951 Cup Final, which Blackpool lost 2–0 to Newcastle United. By contrast, two years later, following the King's death, the young Duke of Edinburgh greets the Blackpool team before the so-called 1953 'Matthews Final', which resulted in a nail-biting 4–3 victory over Bolton Wanderers.

in 1932 for fourteen glorious years before returning to Stoke. He played League football until he was fifty, even turning out for England when he was forty-two, and he picked up eighty-two England caps. He was also the first winner of the uniquely prized Ballon d'Or, awarded to him in 1956, declaring him the world's best footballer.

But Sir Stan always left it to others to talk about his contribution. Sir Walter Winterbottom, former England manager, recalls Sir Stan running riot against a Belgian side in 1947, scoring the last goal in a 5–2 England victory:

> He beat three defenders, the centre-half and the goalkeeper, but it was the reaction of the 70,000 crowd that is etched on my memory. They started a slow hand-clap in time with Stanley's walk as he made his way back for the restart. Then the VIPs joined in, and finally both sets of players as well. It was incredible.

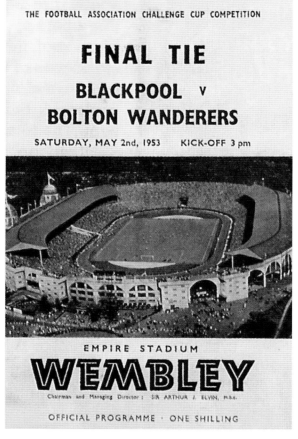

THE FOOTBALL ASSOCIATION CHALLENGE CUP COMPETITION

FINAL TIE

BLACKPOOL v BOLTON WANDERERS

SATURDAY, MAY 2nd, 1953   KICK-OFF 3 pm

EMPIRE STADIUM

WEMBLEY

Chairman and Managing Director : SIR ARTHUR J. ELVIN, M.B.E.

OFFICIAL PROGRAMME · ONE SHILLING

1953 was known as the 'Matthews Final'.

Another memorable Matthews performance was his demolition job on Scotland's full back Harry Haddock at Wembley in 1955. Matthews was involved in every one of England's goals in the 7–2 win. Haddock, who remained one of Stanley's greatest friends, would joke: 'What is Sir Stan's favourite meal? Answer: Haddock … on toast!'

In an age when a single player can command a fee the size of some countries' national debt, one of the greatest ever to grace the Wembley turf was as modest as ever. 'I have no idea how good I was,' he said. 'I never saw me play!' When he died aged eighty-five at home in Stoke-on-Trent in February 2000, the winners' medal from that 1953 FA Cup Final remained his most treasured possession.

*   *   *   *   *

Another memorable, though less glorious, match of 1953 was an international when the unthinkable happened. The English national team, which had only suffered one home defeat

'Mighty Magyar' Ferenc Puskás.

in their entire history, were thrashed by Hungary in what became known as the 'Match of the Century' at Wembley. The Iron Curtain team, dubbed the 'Mighty Magyars', included the legendary Ferenc Puskás, top goalscorer of the twentieth century. He and centre forward Nándor Hidegkuti ran rings around the English, with Hidegkuti scoring after just ninety seconds – the first of a hat-trick. The final score of six goals to three led to a hasty review of England's antiquated training and tactics.

In the FA Cup, West Bromwich Albion lifted the trophy in 1954 with a 3–2 win over Preston North End. And in 1955, Newcastle returned to record their third Cup win in five years, beating Manchester City 3–1, when the great Jackie Milburn opened the scoring after just forty-five seconds. The 'Sky Blues' bounced back the following year in a legendary clash with Birmingham City. The game was remarkable for a heroic performance by Manchester's goalkeeper, Bert Trautmann.

A former German paratrooper who had happily settled in Britain after being taken prisoner of war, Trautmann's story is now legend. He had already acquitted himself nobly the previous year when he became famous as the first German ever to play in an FA Cup Final but his finest moment was the 1956 game against Birmingham City. With seventeen minutes of the match remaining, 'Big Bert'

Bert Trautmann in action. The German former prisoner of war became a hero to Manchester City fans.

dived to snatch the ball from the feet of striker Peter Murphy and was knocked unconscious, still clutching the ball in his hands. He was revived by smelling salts but, without a substitute to replace him, played on for the remaining fifteen minutes in sheer agony, making several further dramatic saves.

Bert Trautmann as a blond pin-up.

When the final whistle blew, Manchester had won 3–1, a victory that could easily have been overturned but for Trautmann. The goalie had to be supported by teammates as he climbed the thirty-nine steps to the Royal Box to collect his winner's medal from the young Queen Elizabeth. Prince Philip asked him why his head was crooked. 'Stiff neck,' he replied. Then he went home to rest, believing the increasing agonies he was suffering were due to muscle strain. Four days later, however, he was persuaded to visit Manchester's Royal Infirmary, where X-rays revealed that he had broken his neck. He was one of the luckiest men alive. Five vertebrae had broken and one of them had split in two. He had survived only because one of the adjoining vertebrae had slammed against it and wedged it into position. Bert spent six months in plaster.

At a time when he should have been counting his blessings, a greater tragedy struck. Trautmann's 5-year-old son was killed by a young driver as his wife watched in horror.

Trautman dives to snatch the ball from the feet of striker Peter Murphy and is knocked unconscious.

She herself died two years later – 'of a broken heart', Bert told the author, 'because she was never the same after that day'. Yet all that Trautmann's Manchester City fans saw in 1965 was a 6ft 2in flaxen-haired hero who was fighting his way back to health after rescuing their FA Cup. It had been feared that he would never play again but he was back in the team within a year, making another 508 appearances for the club.

The next two finals were overshadowed by even more tragedy. Manchester United's much admired 'Busby Babes' played Aston Villa in 1957 but lost 2–1 after their goalkeeper Ray Wood suffered a broken cheek bone early in the game. With substitutes still not allowed, Villa's Peter McParland, who had collided with Wood, scored twice past Jackie Blanchflower, who deputised in goal.

Tommy Taylor, who scored for Manchester, was one of the eight United players who perished in an air disaster just under a year later. On 6 February 1958, a chartered plane crashed on its third attempt to take off from a slush-covered runway at Munich Airport. Aboard were Manchester United's 'Busby Babes', along with officials and journalists. Of the twenty-three who died, England regulars Taylor (nineteen caps), Roger Byrne (thirty-three caps) and Duncan Edwards (eighteen caps) were tragically lost to the game.

It was with an almost entirely new team that United returned to Wembley for the 1958 final. Sadly they went down 2–0 to Bolton Wanderers and could not claim victory as a tribute to their missing teammates. Only two of the United players had been in the previous year's line-up: full back Bill Foulkes and the 20-year-old Bobby Charlton.

One major development at Wembley was the introduction of modern floodlights in 1957, used for the first time at a game between England and the Romanian Under-23s. It allowed midweek games to be played on winter evenings for the first time, instead of during the day when fans were supposed to be at work.

In April 1959, legendary half back Billy Wright notched up his 100th England cap. The Wolverhampton wonder captained England to a 1–0 win over Scotland at Wembley to become the first player in the world to make 100 full international appearances for his country. He had been first chosen to captain England against Ireland eleven years earlier.

The last FA Cup Final of the fifties brought renewed calls for substitutes to be allowed after Nottingham Forest's winger Roy Dwight was carried off with a broken leg. It meant another final where ten men played eleven, but Forest hung on to beat Luton Town 2–1. In the amateur game, Bishop Auckland ended the decade as the most successful club side ever, recording six Wembley appearances in the FA Amateur Cup, which had been first played at Wembley in 1949. They won three times in succession in 1955, 1956 and 1957.

Away from football, there was bad news for speedway fans when weekly racing was suspended in 1957. Part of the problem was that, because of the bends, the cinder track cut across the corners of the grass playing surface. Thus, sections of the hallowed turf had to be frequently removed, stored and replaced so that the two functions could co-exist. Now, as more and more calls were made on the playing surface, from 15,000 to 20,000 individual turfs had to be regularly removed from the pitch. Then, of course, they had to be relaid for the next football fixture. It was with a heavy heart that the decision was taken, especially as the phenomenal speedway crowds of earlier years had helped to keep Wembley in business after the war.

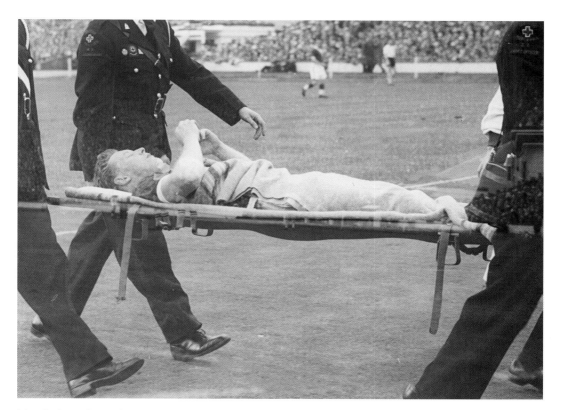

Nottingham Forest's Roy Dwight is carried off with a broken leg in the 1959 Cup Final, reinforcing calls for substitutes to be allowed.

However, speedway had peaked in the 1950s, but gates tumbled towards the end of the decade. A ruinous Entertainment Tax ate away at profits. But it was the loss of Wembley Stadium's founding father and speedway's greatest supporter, Sir Arthur Elvin, that brought an initial end to League racing there. Within a fortnight of his death while on a sunshine cruise in February 1957, the directors announced the withdrawal of the Lions and placed all their riders on the transfer list. Thereafter, Wembley staged only the World Final and occasional Test matches.

If speedway crowds had been fanatical, the followers who flocked to Wembley in May 1955 were positively spiritual – turning out in their tens of thousands for a week of sermons from the great American evangelist Dr Billy Graham. They braved appalling weather to listen to Dr Graham, who said: 'I have never conducted a campaign like this. The thought of 60,000 people a night in the rain will stay in my memory for as long as I live.'

*   *   *   *   *

The prayers of at least some of Dr Billy Graham's followers at Wembley might, without wishing to sound irreverent, have been answered a decade later. For the 1960s were

The Queen looks almost as elated as Danny Blanchflower, the Tottenham Hotspur captain, as he receives the Cup in 1962.

marked by England's capture of the World Cup. The tidal wave of excitement that swept the country during that fantastic 1966 World Cup campaign had been building since the start of the decade when Wembley crowds were treated to some of soccer's finest moments.

For Wembley, it was also the start of a new era. Wembley Stadium Ltd became part of the British Electric Traction group in a deal worth £2,750,000. In 1963, a fibreglass roof and 15,000 new tip-up seats were installed to improve comfort at the Stadium. The giant electronic tote board was also installed.

And something never seen before or since enthralled Wembley – ski jumping. Years before Eddie the Eagle represented Britain in this spectacular sport, the world's greatest Alpine exponents came to Wembley, of all places, to perform. A gigantic ramp, 154 feet (47 metres) high, was constructed within thirty-six hours in time for a two-day (31 May–1 June) event in which forty visiting competitors took part, including the Norwegian national champion Tom Nord and several Olympic medallists. It was one of the most incredible events even Wembley had ever witnessed; artificial snow had been provided by ice-crushing machines and specially treated plastic mats, and the landing area was packed out with straw. As a one-off event, it was certainly a winner with the disbelieving crowds.

On the soccer pitch, the Fabulous Fifties gave way to the Sizzling Sixties as Wolverhampton Wanderers aimed to become the first team this century to record a League and Cup winning double. Wolves won the 1960 cup alright, beating Blackburn Rovers 3–0, courtesy of a Mick McGrath deflected own goal and two strikes from Norman Deeley. But they were denied the League title by one point when they were beaten in the last game of the season – ironically by Tottenham Hotspur.

Spurs, fielding their greatest team of all time, went on to win the elusive, magical double themselves in 1961. Having sewn up the League with eight points to spare – including an incredible thirty-one victories from forty-two games – they went to Wembley to face Leicester City in the FA Cup. The Tottenham faithful had to wait sixty-nine minutes before Bobby Smith smashed a blistering shot past a young Gordon Banks in the Leicester goal. Seven minutes later, Terry Dyson headed home to wrap up a famous 2–0 victory.

Spurs were back the following year, in 1962, determined to keep the Cup in North London. And a plucky Burnley side could do nothing to stop the likes of Jimmy Greaves, Danny Blanchflower, Cliff Jones and Dave Mackay. Greaves, who rattled in a hat-trick for England in a 9–3 rout of Scotland in the previous year, was on target again after just three minutes to send Spurs on their way to a 3–1 win. The Scots returned in April 1963 and got their revenge with a 2–1 win, midfield maestro Jim Baxter scoring both goals. Disappointed but unfazed, England then played host to the exotic talents of Brazil and were happy with a 1–1 draw. It was a taste of the excitement to come, however, for Wembley crowds. In Late May, the European Cup Final came to England for the first time with the Italian champions AC Milan taking on Benfica of Portugal and winning 2–1.

Our own domestic Cup Final of 1963 was delayed until 25 May because of a heavy fixture backlog caused by a particularly severe winter. Manchester United, with Denis Law, Pat Crerand and Johnny Giles, saw off the challenge of Leicester City. David Herd beat Gordon Banks twice, and Law added another as United ran out 3–1 winners.

The spicy flavours of the wider world of soccer were simmering again in October when the Football Association celebrated its centenary with a game against the Rest of the World. Mighty Russian Lev Yashin was in goal with the great Eusébio of Portugal, Alfredo Di Stéfano of Spain, Raymond Kopa of France, Djalma Santos of Brazil, Francisco Gento of Spain and Scotland's Denis Law all in the same side. It was a feast of football, especially as England won 2–1 with goals from Terry Paine and Jimmy Greaves – the latter by now treating Wembley almost as his 'home' ground! The year ended with Wembley's first fully floodlit international, Greaves scoring four times as England beat Northern Ireland 8–3. It went towards his amazing record as First Division top scorer six times from 1959 to 1969. In those six seasons he scored 212 goals.

During 1963, Wembley enjoyed a £500,000 facelift, which saw the distinctive all-round roof installed, using fibreglass panels on the inner 36 feet. It gave cover over both ends for the first time. Out of the ground's 100,000 visitor capacity, 44,000 were now seated.

*   *   *   *   *

Boxing made a return to Wembley on 18 June 1963, for the first time since Jack Petersen's 1935 defeat, as another great British heavyweight hope, the much loved Henry Cooper, climbed into the ring to face a brash young American invader by the name of Cassius Clay.

Eliminating Contest for the

HEAVYWEIGHT CHAMPIONSHIP OF THE WORLD

Wembley Stadium
Tuesday 18th June, 1963

OFFICIAL PROGRAMME TWO SHILLINGS & SIXPENCE

Cassius Clay

Henry Cooper

Cockney Cooper, Europe's top heavyweight for most of the sixties, was already the nation's favourite sporting son when he made his way through the cheering ranks of his supporters and into the ring, set up in the middle of the Stadium. This night, the whole nation was behind him. 'They wanted me to knock Clay's block off,' he said later. 'He'd

The most famous punch thrown in a British boxing ring ... as Henry Cooper floors Cassius Clay.

Cassius Clay hits the canvas just three seconds before the end of Round Four. Would he rise again?

been telling everyone that he was the greatest. He'd made up nursery rhymes telling what he was going to do to me. He was getting right up everybody's nose.'

In the pre-fight hype, the 'Louisville Lip', as the fast-talking Clay was known, had been taunting: 'If he give me jive, he fall in five.' He had jokingly complained:

> The ring ain't large enough. Cooper don't have enough running room. The fans will be booing after the third round because I will be playing with a clown. I'm gonna whup him like I'm his daddy. I'm going to whup him like he stole something.

Typically, Cooper had remained unruffled throughout all the taunting, saying: 'He's just selling tickets.'

When, on the night, Clay made his regal entrance into the Stadium wearing a cardboard crown, it goaded the fans even more. But it looked as if the visitor's boasts were nothing more than hot air as Cooper initially took the fight to Clay to win the opening two rounds. He was also going well in round three until he emerged from one close range encounter with blood suddenly pouring from a cut over his left eye. Despite the injury, Cooper's corner allowed him 'just one more round'.

Just three seconds from the end of round four came the magic moment: an explosion of power, the most famous punch ever thrown in a British ring. The packed crowd of 44,000 leaped to their feet in delirium as 'Enery's 'Ammer', his famed thunderbolt left hook, landed flush on Clay's jaw and sent him sprawling on the ropes and then crashing to the canvas. For a few heart-stopping seconds, it seemed as if the whole course of heavyweight history would be changed.

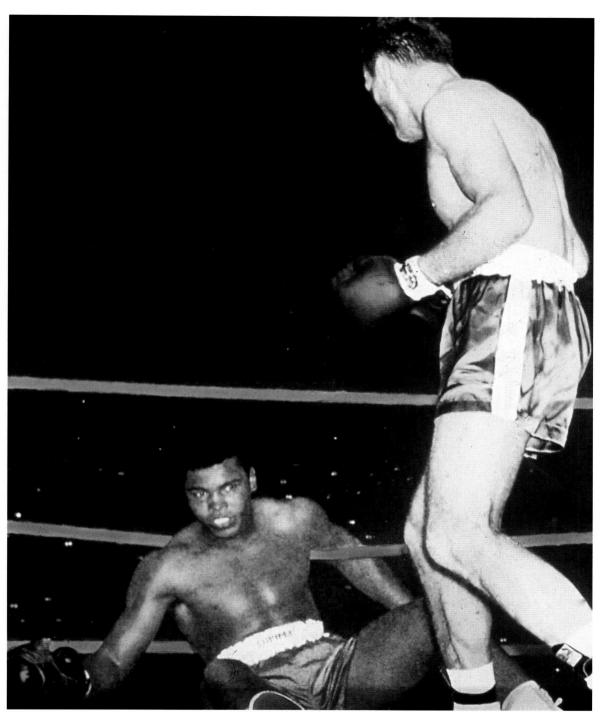

Cooper towers above an obviously dazed Clay. He later said: 'That guy hit me so hard he didn't only shake me – he shook my relatives in Africa!'

End of a dream for 'Our 'Enery' ... By Round Five, Cooper's cut eye was so badly split that the referee had to call the match to a close.

As Clay hauled himself dazedly up, however, the bell gave him precious sanctuary. The normal one-minute interval was more than doubled after the string of his glove was mysteriously cut. Refreshed and rejuvenated, he came out in round five to blast away at Cooper, splitting his face so badly that the referee had to end what had become a bloodbath.

So, sadly for 'Our 'Enery', Clay's predicted result had come true – but only just. As Cooper recalled:

> A guy's eyes tell you everything, and when I looked down on him he just had a blank look. If the punch had landed twenty seconds sooner, who knows what might have happened. Still, you can't change history. And I'm not grumbling – I dined out on it ever since!

Clay's own comment on his near defeat was: 'That guy Cooper hit me so hard he didn't only shake me – he shook my relatives in Africa!' Clay went on to win the World Heavyweight title eight months later, before changing his name to Muhammad Ali and writing his own supreme chapter in sporting history.

* * * * *

Another sporting hero, even more loved than Henry Cooper if that is possible, graced Wembley the following year. The late great Bobby Moore led out West Ham in 1964 as they made their first appearance in a Cup Final since Wembley's very first fixture, the 'White Horse Final' of 1923. Also notably on the score sheet as the Hammers beat Preston North End 3–2 was Geoff Hurst. As they climbed to the Royal Box after that game, neither he nor Moore could have imagined the circumstances in which they would be ascending those steps again in both of the two following years.

In 1965, the great Leeds United side of Norman Hunter, Johnny Giles, Billy Bremner and Jack Charlton looked as if they were heading for a League and Cup double. But in the Cup Final they were up against a powerful Liverpool line-up including Chris Lawler, Ron Yeats, Tommy Smith, Ian Callaghan, Roger Hunt and Ian St John. It was not to be Leeds' year. They lost the final 2–1 thanks to an extra time winner from St John and missed out on the League title on goal difference to Manchester United.

Rugby League followers reckoned that the 1965 Challenge Cup Final between Wigan and Hunslet was one of the greatest games ever seen. And Wigan's captain, Eric Ashton, was undoubtedly one of its greatest exponents. The game kicked off sensationally as Hunslet scored from a penalty before their opponents had even touched the ball, but Wigan stormed their way back to a 20–16 win in a thrilling finale.

Throughout the latter part of the twentieth century, Eric Ashton and Wembley Stadium seemed to go together like fish and chips. He appeared there for a Challenge Cup Final eleven times either as a player, a coach or chairman of a club – a record unsurpassed in League history.

THE RUGBY LEAGUE CHALLENGE CUP COMPETITION

FINAL TIE
HUNSLET
V
WIGAN

SATURDAY, MAY 8th 1965 Kick-off 3 p.m.

WEMBLEY
EMPIRE STADIUM

OFFICIAL PROGRAMME - - - ONE SHILLING

One of Rugby League's greatest ever games.

Ashton captained Wigan a record six times at the Twin Towers, in 1958, 1959, 1961, 1963, 1956 and 1966. He coached them in 1965, 1966 and 1970. He then coached great rivals St Helens in 1976 and 1978 before returning as chairman of Saints for the 1996 and 1997 finals against the Bradford Bulls.

Other Wigan stars of the sixties who helped make Wembley Stadium the southern home of this traditionally 'northern' sport included Shaun Edwards, who played in no fewer than ten finals, and Neil Fox, who scored a record twenty points in the 1960 final against Wakefield Trinity. The other Rugby League legend of the time was the St Helens, Leigh, Warrington and Great Britain superstar Alex Murphy, who played in four Cup Finals and won the lot, scoring a try in St Helens' famous 1961 win over arch rivals Wigan. After the 1966 final, the man known as 'Murphy the Mouth' sent this telegram to the losers: 'Roses are red, violets are blue, St Helens 21, Wigan 2.'

International soccer action thrilled the nation in May 1965 as West Ham played Munich in Wembley's first European Cup Winners' Cup Final. A typically stylish performance from Bobby Moore helped to unsettle the impressive looking Germans and in attack Martin Peters delivered a foretaste of things to come, laying on the second goal for Alan Sealey as the Hammers gained a fine 2–0 win.

Moore, who was said by no less a judge than Pele to be 'the best defender in the world', always reckoned that this was his finest club match. He said some years later:

> Winning the World Cup in 1966 has to be the pinnacle of my career but the Cup Winners' Cup victory over Munich is the game that gave me most satisfaction at club level. It was the best of both worlds – playing with your mates, guys who you trained with week in and week out, and in front of your own fans in a major final on the international stage. Wonderful.

Eric Ashton, who captained Wigan six times at Wembley, holds aloft Rugby League's Challenge Cup.

In 1966, in all areas of English soccer, the skill, the style and the confidence was apparent and all around the country anticipation was growing for the great event ahead. Before the World Cup began in 1966, however, there was the little matter of the FA Cup to be decided – a War of the Roses clash between Everton and Sheffield Wednesday. It was a thrilling battle with Sheffield taking a two-goal lead only to see a brilliant Everton fightback. Two goals from Mike Trebilcock and another by Derek Temple ten minutes from time gave the Merseysiders a deserved win.

*   *   *   *   *

The sixties were, of course, dominated by the greatest glory English soccer has ever known – winning the World Cup in front of a fanatical home crowd. When Bobby Moore climbed the thirty-nine steps to the Royal Box on 30 July 1966 after disposing of West Germany 4–2, he led ten men whose names are indelibly etched in our national consciousness: Gordon Banks, George Cohen, Ray Wilson, Nobby Styles, Martin Peters, Alan Ball, Roger Hunt, Geoff Hurst and Bobby and Jackie Charlton. For the first and only time since the competition began, English players were able to hold the solid gold Jules Rimet trophy aloft in triumph as undisputed champions of the world.

The result had been confidently promised by former Southampton full back Alfred Ramsey, who had been given the job of England manager in 1962 after the team failed to beat Brazil in the World Cup in Chile. But victory had not always seemed so certain to the anxious crowds witnessing 1966's early events at Wembley, which was the venue for all of England's fixtures in the tournament. The home team got off to a lacklustre start with a 0–0 draw against Uruguay, and when they took to the field to play Mexico in the second

WORLD CHAMPIONSHIP
JULES RIMET CUP

Final

ENGLAND v WEST GERMANY

SATURDAY · JULY 30 · 1966
EMPIRE STADIUM
SOUVENIR PROGRAMME WEMBLEY PRICE 2/6

match the tension was almost tangible. Bobby Charlton brought the country to its feet in the thirty-seventh minute, rampaging deep into Mexican territory from his own half before unleashing an unstoppable right foot shot to give England the lead. Roger Hunt added a second. The performance was still far from convincing, however. In the final group game against France, Hunt put England ahead, snapping up a rebound when Jack Charlton's header hit the post. With Nobby Stiles fearsomely aggressive in midfield, Hunt added a second from Ian Callaghan's cross.

The quarter-finals pitted England against Argentina and a game of bone-crunching tackles, dissent and off-the-ball incidents unfolded. Argentine captain Antonio Rattin was sent off, gaining instant notoriety, and Geoff Hurst, making his World Cup debut, headed the only goal of the game, gaining instant acclaim.

The game that made history ... Bobby Moore's England team line-up for the 1966 World Cup.

Bobby Moore presents the England team to the Queen at the opening match.

England lined up against Portugal in the semi-final – often described as the best game of the whole competition. Both teams were sheer class but the difference was made by Bobby Charlton. He scored both goals as England took the lead. However, everyone had their hearts in their mouths in the final few minutes after Portugal pulled one back when the great Eusébio took a penalty kick nine minutes from time to make the final score 2–1.

With West Germany beating Italy 2–1 in their semi-final, the stage was set for an epic clash on 30 July. No one who saw it, among the 93,000 in the Stadium or the millions watching at home, will ever forget it …

Germany were first to score after Helmut Haller seized on an uncharacteristic lapse by full back Ray Wilson to fire home a shot that cannoned off Jack Charlton's foot. Five minutes later, Geoff Hurst bagged an equaliser, heading home a free kick taken exquisitely by Bobby Moore. From then on, England seemed to swarm all over the pitch – Alan Ball was unstoppable, Moore was majestic and Bobby Charlton outshone even the stylish Franz Beckenbauer as England looked for victory.

With twelve minutes to go, Germany failed to scramble clear a corner from Ball. Martin Peters, another of the West Ham contingent in the England side, calmly smacked it into the back of the net and the Cup was as good as won. Until, that is, Wolfgang Weber forced an equaliser from a disputed free kick only seconds from the end of normal time.

Handed the Jules Rimet Trophy by the Queen, Moore kisses the cup that all England dreamed of.

More kisses from Moore, before (*below*) handing the Cup to Geoff Hurst while Nobby Stiles does a victory dance.

There was further uproar as England claimed Germany's Haller handled the ball as it was knocked across the box.

Ten minutes into extra time came the goal everyone still talks about. Geoff Hurst took a pass from Ball and unleashed a rocket, which hit the underside of the crossbar, bounced down and was then kicked away. Did it cross the line? Was it a goal? Roger Hunt, who was on hand to knock it in if it hadn't already crossed the line, thought it was. He threw up his arms and turned away in delight. Swiss referee Gottfried Dienst thought it was, but wasn't sure. He consulted his Russian linesman, Tofik Bahramov, who was in no doubt. The 'goal' was given and England were 3–2 up.

England held on, and as the seconds ticked away, Hurst broke free down the left. His amazing drive that followed created another of the world's most memorable goals – encapsulated forever by the commentary of the BBC's Kenneth Wolstenholme, who said: 'Some people are on the pitch. They think it's all over … It is now!'

Emotional recollections from some of the champions of that day included those from England's hat-trick hero Geoff Hurst, who said: 'The noise coming from the Wembley crowd was such a crescendo it made the hairs stand up on the back of my neck. It still does thinking about it. It seemed like the whole country was there.'

Captain Bobby Moore shares the moment of glory with the architect of England's victory, Alf Ramsey.

Bobby Charlton said:

> When the final whistle went I was looking round at everybody. My brother Jack went down on his knees. Most of the others were jumping with delight. I got quite moved and there were a few tears, which I'm not ashamed of. We were the best team in the world at that time and we had just proved it. It was the biggest event that ever happened in English sporting history.

Alan Ball said: 'It was the greatest day of my life, simple as that. We didn't play for money. It was the glory of winning the World Cup for England that burned in us all.'

Modest captain Bobby Moore probably had the least to say. It was left to Alf Ramsey to sum up the qualities of the man who led England to glory. Ramsay called him:

> My captain, my leader, my right-hand man. He was the spirit and the heartbeat of the team. A cool, calculating footballer I could trust with my life. He was the supreme professional, the best I ever worked with. Without him England would never have won the World Cup.

There is one strange footnote to be added to the saga of the 1966 World Cup. Four months before the final, the Jules Rimet Trophy was stolen from a London exhibition, the thief hoping for a handsome ransom. He failed and was apprehended. The Cup was found under a hedge by a dog named Pickles. Poor Pickles later strangled himself with his own lead while chasing a cat.

*   *   *   *   *

With the quality of English football at an all-time peak, Spurs and Chelsea met for the 1967 Cup Final for the first all-London clash since the competition began in 1872. Spurs were making their fifth appearance in the final – they had won the previous four – and they were not to be denied this time either, beating the Blues 2–1. It was, incidentally, the first final allowing substitutes to be used.

Another soccer trophy came to Wembley in this year and has been played for ever since under various names: the League Cup. It had previously been a two-legged affair played at the two clubs' home grounds but now, with a UEFA Cup place at stake, Wembley was naturally deemed to be the most fitting venue. Queen's Park Rangers from the Third Division were inspired by Rodney Marsh to beat high-flying West Bromwich Albion in a thrilling 3–2 final.

The 1968 FA Cup Final between West Brom and Everton saw a dull ninety minutes and a game settled after three minutes of extra time by West Brom's Jeff Astle.

There was excitement aplenty later the same May, however, when Manchester United played the mighty Benfica for the honour of winning the European Cup. Benfica fielded half of the Portuguese World Cup team, including 'Black Panther' Eusébio da Silva Ferreira, and they arrived with the tournament's best ever defensive record. United broke the ice when Bobby Charlton flicked a cross into the net early in the second half. 'My first header for about ten years,' he joked afterwards, 'and if I hadn't been going bald it wouldn't have gone in.' Benfica equalised, and in extra time, the great George Best dazzled the Portuguese defence and virtually walked the ball into the net. Moments later, Brian Kidd, celebrating his nineteenth birthday, headed home from Charlton's corner, and as the Reds romped towards a famous victory, Charlton scored the fourth with one of his most fantastic strikes.

Chelsea goalkeeper Peter Bonetti dives at the feet of Spurs' Jimmy Greaves to save his goal during the 1967 FA Cup Final.

Ron 'Chopper' Harris of Chelsea tackles Jimmy Greaves in the 1967 Cup Final. Greaves had the last laugh as Tottenham won 2–1.

In 1968, what Wembley's supporters came to view as 'sacrilege' took place when the Royal International Horse Show was staged on the hallowed turf. The pitch, which was originally designed to accommodate only two matches a year, was already being severely tested by the number of events taking place on it. Show jumping proved one too many.

Lowly Swindon Town turned the form book upside down when they faced Arsenal in the League Cup in 1969. With the pitch in a terrible state, the Third Division side from Wiltshire turned on a cavalier performance and two extra time goals from Don Rogers gave them the last laugh over their aristocratic big city rivals. Rogers' second, an incredible run from inside his own half that ended with him waltzing around Arsenal keeper Bob Wilson, immediately entered Wembley and West Country folklore.

The summer of 1969 was unusually wet and when the Horse Show returned – fortunately after Manchester City had beaten Leicester City 1–0 in the FA Cup – it turned the pitch into a quagmire. This meant that the Swinging Sixties gave way to what were, initially at least, the Soggy Seventies ...

*   *   *   *   *

Thanks to the previous year's Horse Show, the first Cup Final of the seventies saw Leeds United and Chelsea ploughing through the worst conditions the Stadium has ever known. The score was 2–2 at the whistle but, due to the state of the pitch, both teams were too tired to create anything in extra time, making it the first FA Cup Final to require a replay since 1912. It took place at Old Trafford and, after more extra time, Chelsea took the Cup back to Stamford Bridge with a 2–1 win.

Horses for the wrong courses! Leeds and Chelsea plough through the quagmire caused by the previous year's horse show.

One sport that did not need any turf at all was speedway, which made a brief comeback when a Wembley based millionaire businessman, Bernard Cottrell, and a former international rider, Trevor Redmond, reintroduced League racing in 1970. The Lions team was re-formed and for two years the sport received its best support in the country from the Wembley crowds. Ove Fundin, the Swedish rider who won four of his five world titles at Wembley, captained the new Lions but the practicalities of taking up the turf in the corners of the pitch to accommodate the speedway track meant that the return was short-lived. The last League meeting passed without ceremony on 25 September 1971, with a home victory over London rivals Wimbledon. The World Final continued to be staged at the Stadium on a three-year cycle until 1981. In the last ever speedway meeting at Wembley, American Bruce Penhall, who later went on to star in the TV motorcycle cop series *CHiPs*, was crowned world champion. The chequered flag had been lowered on the sport's final race.

The FA Cup Final in 1971 saw Arsenal aiming for a delightful double – exactly ten years after their North London neighbours Tottenham had achieved the same feat. Arsenal manager Bertie Mee and coach Don Howe had created a formidable unit, captained by Frank McLintock, powered by George Graham and George Armstrong, given flair by

Peter Simpson of Arsenal clears from Steve Heighway of Liverpool in the 1971 Cup Final.

Charlie George and Ray Kennedy, and backed by the safe hands of Bob Wilson in goal. Incredibly they played sixty-four fixtures that season and a victory over Spurs handed them the League title only five days before the final.

The Liverpool team lined up against them was managed by Bill Shankly and contained the striking partnership of John Toshack and Steve Heighway, the stylish Emlyn Hughes, hard man Tommy Smith and the top class goalkeeping skills of Ray Clemence. A pulsating ninety minutes produced much to admire but no goals, so extra time ensued. Heighway opened the scoring two minutes into the extra half hour but Arsenal equalised through substitute Eddie Kelly – the first ever 'super sub' to score in a final. Fighting exhaustion, the Gunners battled on until, with eight minutes to go, Charlie George released a fearsome shot that left Clemence no chance. The pictures of an ecstatic George lying flat on his back with his arms outstretched became a symbol of a great 2–1 victory.

Dutch master Johan Cruyff's Ajax of Amsterdam were the visitors in June as Wembley hosted its third European Cup Final. Thanks to the silky skills of the European Footballer of the Year, Ajax were never in trouble as they beat Panathinaikos of Athens 2–0. The scorer of both goals was Dik van Dijk – no relation to the film star who appeared in *Mary Poppins*!

As mentioned earlier, Rugby legend Alex Murphy played in four Cup Finals and won the lot but his proudest moment almost passed him by altogether. There were just fifteen minutes of the 1971 final left and Leigh – coached by Murphy and rank outsiders to knock over the favourites Leeds – were leading by a staggering 17–2. Suddenly Murphy went to ground. Referee Billy Thompson stepped in and Leeds' Syd Hynes became the first Rugby League player to take the long, lonely walk down the tunnel, sent off for an alleged butt. Hynes supporters claimed that the crafty 'victim' took a dive. Murphy, the impish genius of his day who later denied any chicanery, was stretchered off to the dressing room to return a few minutes later to join in the celebrations as little town Leigh lifted the Challenge Cup with a remarkable 24–7 victory. Murphy, true to his billing in the greatest Rugby League theatre in the world, lifted the Lance Todd Trophy as Man of the Match.

Above: Young star: Alex Murphy's Saints after beating Wigan 21–2 in 1966.

Right: Veteran: Murphy with the key to Wembley when the boss of St Helens.

Prime Minister Harold Wilson applauds as Alex Murphy lifts the Challenge Cup in 1974.

In a tribute to the venue, Murphy recalled:

> That day was the proudest of my career. Leeds thought they had only to turn up to lift the trophy and the bookies made them 5–1 on to do just that. But Wembley is something extra special to a Rugby League player. Winning there is the greatest feeling you can ever have in sport.

Murphy left Leigh shortly afterwards to become player-coach at Warrington. The 1973–74 season was the club's most successful, winning the Challenge Cup, Captain Morgan Trophy, John Player Trophy and Club Merit Trophy. Murphy's highlight came in May 1974 when he coached, captained and played stand-off half in a 24–9 victory over Featherstone Rovers in front of a 77,500 Wembley crowd. He retired as a player shortly after but remained on as coach of the club until 1978.

*   *   *   *   *

Something that was new and exciting – but would become a familiar part of Wembley life – happened at the Stadium in 1972. The first rock concert was staged on Saturday, 5 August. At the time, it was the biggest rock 'n' roll show the world had ever seen, with Bill Haley and the Comets, Little Richard and Chuck Berry headlining the show. It was a twelve-hour marathon of classic rock, with 10,000 watts of power pumping up the volume. To prevent damage to the turf, Wembley helped to design a new type of plastic covering that allowed people to stand on the grass without harming it. The protective shield also allowed the grass to breathe naturally underneath it.

For trivia buffs, the first band ever to play the Stadium was The Houseshakers, followed by the first solo performer – the late Billy Fury. It was the start of a magnificent tradition of open-air performances from some of the world's biggest music business names. Crosby, Stills, Nash and Young appeared at Wembley in front of 70,000 fans in 1974. Huge numbers turned out to hear The Beach Boys in 1977 and The Who in 1979. Simon and Garfunkel, The Rolling Stones, Elton John, Bob Dylan and Bruce Springsteen all filled the Stadium in the early eighties. And, of course, the pinnacle of Wembley's musical history was to occur on 13 July 1985, when Live Aid united the world.

Wembley's first rock concert was staged in 1972.

*　　　*　　　*　　　*　　　*

Back in the world of sport, 1972 saw West Germany gain revenge over England for their World Cup defeat six years earlier. With the emerging talents of the great Franz Beckenbauer, they comfortably strolled to a 3–1 victory in a European Nations Cup quarter-final. England still had Banks, Ball, Hunt, Moore and Peters in their line-up from the 1966 side and the margin of defeat was an uncomfortable reminder that one can't live on past glories.

It was also the year of the FA's Centenary Cup Final, and the first week in May saw Arsenal return to face Leeds. This time, however, it was Leeds who had sight of a League

The Leeds defence can only watch as Ian Porterfield scores the Cup winner for Sunderland in 1973.

and Cup double. A long, hard season left them needing one point away to Wolves – but the game was scheduled to be played just two days after the Cup Final. With Billy Bremner, Johnny Giles, Norman Hunter and Peter Lorimer on top form, Leeds just about edged Arsenal out of the game, Allan Clarke – who needed a painkilling injection before the game – scoring the only goal after fifty-three minutes.

Perhaps the long struggle was just too much, because Leeds went down to Wolves the following Monday. Things didn't improve, either, for Alf Ramsey's England that year. They lost 0–1 to Northern Ireland for the first time since 1957.

The Cup Final of 1973 produced one of the biggest upsets the competition had ever known when Second Division Sunderland faced a mighty Leeds side. Every player in the Yorkshire team had been an international and they had finished in the top three of the First Division for six years running. Yet Sunderland beat them 1–0. Ian Porterfield scored a goal the Sunderland fans will remember forever but the real hero of the day was their goalkeeper, Jim Montgomery, who pulled off a string of fine saves – most notably two together from Trevor Cherry's header and Peter Lorimer's blistering follow-up drive, which Montgomery miraculously tipped over the bar with seemingly telescopic arms.

That 1973 result was followed by two more similar shocks – when Southampton beat Manchester United in 1976, and unfancied Ipswich beat Arsenal in 1978. And those upsets would have surprising implications for every side that played at Wembley in the years ahead. Deeply superstitious as footballers are, someone realised that the winning teams had all shared the same dressing room – and it wasn't the one England had made their own until this quirky statistic came to light. Statisticians began to check through the

Second Division Sunderland beat mighty Leeds in the 1973 Cup Final after Ian Porterfield scored the only goal. It was one of the biggest upsets the competition has ever known.

records and found that, in recent years, nine times out of ten the victors had used the same dressing rooms. After that, England moved to the south dressing room and the dressing room to the north of the players' tunnel gained the unenviable reputation of being the 'unlucky' one. On Cup Final day, the team whose name began nearest to the letter A was allocated the north dressing room.

Former Arsenal and Scotland great Bob Wilson reckoned that some games were won and lost when the teams left the sanctuary of the changing area and waited in the tunnel for the signal to walk out onto the pitch. As they emerged, the 'Wembley roar' of 80,000 fans hit them and, said Wilson: 'They either stick out their chest and remember all they've dreamt about or their head drops into their shoulders and they get stage fright. Whatever happens, games can be decided there and then.'

Maybe that's what happened to England's 1973 World Cup hopes when they played Poland in October. They needed a win to qualify for the finals but could only manage a 1–1 draw in this fateful and never-to-be-forgotten encounter. Brian Clough had unwisely described Poland's keeper Jan Tomaszewski as 'a clown' but the goalie had the last laugh, pulling off many fine saves. The only time he was beaten was by Allan Clarke from the penalty spot. As England pressed forward, and the crowd generated an electric atmosphere, Clarke, Mick Channon and Tony Currie were also denied by Tomaszewski. Even in the last seconds,

Jubilant Liverpool captain Emlyn Hughes about to accept the FA Cup from Princess Anne after Liverpool's 3–0 victory over Newcastle United in the 1974 final. It was a highlight of a decade of success for Liverpool, the year after winning the UEFA Cup – to be followed by three league titles, two European Cups and a second UEFA Cup.

England had an effort cleared off the line. When the whistle blew, a capacity 100,000 crowd overcame their shattered dreams and loudly showed their support for a terrific performance.

In 1974, there were no shocks, just thrills as the well-oiled machine that was Liverpool FC demolished Newcastle United 3–0 to lift the Cup. Shankly's 'Red Army' were powered by the almost nuclear force that was Kevin Keegan, together with Emlyn Hughes, John Toshack, Brian Hall, Alec Lindsay and the imposing Tommy Smith at the back. Keegan netted twice, and Heighway slotted one in between them.

At the start of the season, a new trophy joined the impressive array of silverware fought for annually at Wembley. It was the FA Charity Shield, traditionally played between the league champions and FA Cup winners of the previous season as a curtain-raiser to the new campaign. Liverpool added the trophy to their impressive collection after a penalty shoot-out following their 1–1 draw with Leeds. But the match is mostly remembered for Billy Bremner and Kevin Keegan being jointly dismissed from the field by referee Bob Matthewson for a second-half brawl. The two players, who angrily tore off their shirts as they left the pitch, were accused of bringing football into disrepute. Their behaviour led to questions in Parliament. Keegan later admitted:

> I've played in losing Cup Finals but my saddest memory is being sent off with dear old Billy Bremner. I think we paid the penalty for being the next to get caught up in something at a time when the referee thought he was losing control of things. It's a very long, lonely walk to the players' tunnel – that's what stands out in my memory the most. It's ever such a short walk when you're winning but it's a long, long way when you're sent off.

Things began looking up again for England – maybe the change of dressing room really worked – because in

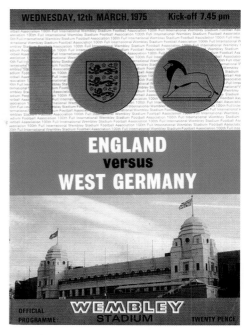

In a 1975 friendly, England beat then world champions West Germany 2–0.

In the 1975 Cup Final, West Ham's 2–0 victory over Fulham is celebrated by Alan Taylor and Bobby Gould.

The ball flashes past Manchester United keeper Alex Stepney to give Second Division Southampton victory in the 1976 FA Cup Final. Thanks to that single goal by Bobby Stokes, Southampton became the second Second Division club in four years to win the trophy.

Liverpool's Ray Kennedy heads goalwards in 1977 – but Alex Stepney saves, allowing Manchester United to record a famous 2–1 victory.

March 1975 they beat the then world champions West Germany 2–0 with goals from Colin Bell and Malcolm MacDonald. This year also saw another all-London Cup Final with Fulham taking on West Ham. It wasn't a classic and the Hammers went home with the trophy thanks to a 2–0 win.

Second Division Southampton's win over Manchester United the following year was, like Sunderland's earlier victory, celebrated around the country. Wembley fans always love an underdog and, as Saints manager Lawrie McMenemy quipped: 'We are the country lads who are not supposed to be able to find our way out of the tunnel.' But, with just seven minutes of time left, Bobby Stokes beat Alex Stepney for the only goal of the game.

The trend to turn footballers into walking advertising billboards began around this time. England's strip gained fancy flashes in 1976 and the maker's Admiral logo was put on the shirts.

The great Liverpool side of the seventies were lined up for a unique treble in 1977. They had just clinched the League title after a long hard season, were facing rivals Manchester United in the FA Cup Final and four days after that they were due to meet Borussia Mönchengladbach in the European Cup Final. With Jimmy Case, Terry McDermott and Ray Kennedy in midfield and the non-stop enterprise of Keegan up front, many believed they could actually pull it off. Manchester's Red Devils, however, were determined to spoil the party and, mainly during a magic five minutes of pile-driving football, shot two goals to Liverpool's one. Great character was then shown by Liverpool, led by Bob Paisley, in pulling themselves off the floor and delivering a night of magic to lift the European Cup with a thrilling 3–1 win over Borussia in Rome.

In the League Cup of that year, it seemed as though nothing could separate Aston Villa and Everton. After a 0–0 draw at Wembley, they fought out a 1–1 replay at Hillsborough after extra time. The second replay, at old Trafford, also needed extra time before Villa ran out 3–2 winners.

It was important to fans that England produced the best club side in Europe because three months earlier the national side had been given a lesson in footballing professionalism by an amazing foreign side. This was the night Holland came to town for a friendly and painted it orange with the supreme craft of Johan Cruyff, the flair of Johan Neeskens and the swagger of Johnny Rep. Cruyff was the inevitable star of arguably the most demonstrative display by an away team against England since the Hungarians of 1953. Wembley had stood to applaud the Dutch players from the pitch at half-time as they handed Don Revie's side a lesson in the power of Total Football.

Revie, recognised as one of the most thorough managers of all time, had recently compiled a 300-point dossier on how to cope with a major Wembley match, dealing with everything from psychology to seating arrangements. It did him no good whatsoever. Holland completed the friendly 2–0 up and the manner and style of their win gained unstinting praise. England's failure, on the other hand, earned scorn, best summed up by respected soccer critic Jeff Powell, who wrote:

> England joined the rest of the second-raters in the gutter of world football last night. The last dregs of self-respect drained away to the accompaniment of Wembley's new theme tune, *What a load of rubbish*. To be one of 90,000 Englishmen in this once impregnable stadium was a demoralising experience. For England were not merely beaten for the first time by Holland … they were torn apart.

The agony and the ecstasy ... *Top left*: Gordon McQueen of Manchester United punches towards the Arsenal goal in the 1979 Cup Final. *Top right*: It's agony for losers Brian Greenhoff and Steve Coppell as Arsenal win 3–2. *Below*: By contrast, the Gunners celebrate ecstatically, with Graham Rix throwing his arms in the air while Brian Talbot offers a prayer of thanks.

In June, it was Scotland's turn to celebrate when a 2–1 win gave them their first Wembley victory over England for ten years. Asa Hartford, Lou Macari and Don Masson dominated midfield and Gordon McQueen and Kenny Dalglish knocked in the goals. Sadly, the Scots' joy turned into near hysteria. Thousands of hooligans flooded the pitch, dug up large chunks of the turf to take home as souvenirs and even smashed the crossbar of one goal into matchwood. It was an infamously black day for Scottish soccer, even though the Scottish FA presented Wembley with a new set of goalposts. But rumblings of discontent had begun, which eventually saw the 'Home International' meetings between the two banned.

There were brighter times ahead, though, when the boys from Brazil arrived in April 1978 to entertain the crowd. England were happy with a 1–1 draw, Keegan equalising with a free kick worthy of the visiting South Americans.

The FA Cup Final the following month was Wembley's fiftieth and marked the start of three consecutive appearances by Arsenal. Unfashionable Ipswich Town were the opponents but manager Bobby Robson was soon to prove that the wilds of East Anglia could produce football every bit as competitive as their city slicker counterparts. Roger Osborne settled it for Ipswich with the only goal of the game.

Four days later, Liverpool were back at Wembley, not for any domestic trophy but in a glorious bid to retain the European Cup. Liverpool dominated but couldn't turn their possession into goals as opponents Bruges packed their defence. With twenty-five minutes remaining, however, Dalglish created an opening, collected a sweet pass from Graeme Souness and chipped the Bruges keeper for a magnificent goal. It was enough to win the Cup – but only just. Just before the end, Phil Thompson saved the day by clearing off the Liverpool goal line with keeper Clemence stranded.

Lifting the Cup was a magical moment for skipper Emlyn Hughes, whose glittering career had more highlights than most. He recalled:

> I managed to get to Wembley more than forty times, captaining both Liverpool and England. Each visit was like entering a magical world. I played in three FA Cup Finals and a League Cup Final, but being in the European Cup side when we beat FC Bruges 1–0 in front of a 92,000 crowd is something I will take to my grave with me.

Even a stadium as great as Wembley had rarely seen more drama than in the 1979 FA Cup Final, when Arsenal returned to face Manchester United. Brian Talbot, who joined the Gunners from the Cup-winning Ipswich side, opened the scoring after twelve minutes and Frank Stapelton's header just before half-time looked to have put Arsenal comfortably in the driving seat. They maintained their advantage until, with less than four minutes to go, big Gordon McQueen rose to head home a centre from the other United giant, Joe Jordan. With the crowd on their feet, Sammy McIlroy waltzed through the Arsenal defence just two minutes later to roll home an equaliser. And still it wasn't over … Liam Brady, contemplating extra time, took the ball back into the United half as the last few seconds ticked away. Suddenly Graham Rix sprinted

40 yards and centred for Alan Sunderland, who calmly put the ball in the net. United were stunned – and Arsenal were the Cup winners.

$$* \quad * \quad * \quad * \quad *$$

The Twin Towers witnessed some extraordinary spectacles in the 1980s. It was the decade of glitz and glamour, during which Wembley hit the headlines as often for its extravagant rock and royal events as it did for its sporting highlights. Princess Diana lit up the Stadium when she visited. Kings of pop, like The Rolling Stones, drew the most colourful of crowds. And even Pope Paul II celebrated Mass at the cathedral of sport!

But it wasn't fun for everyone ... Arsenal left heartbroken when they returned in 1980 for a record-breaking three consecutive FA Cup Final appearances. They hoped that it would prove third time lucky for them but the underdogs of the day, Second Division West Ham United, spoiled the party. Trevor Brooking notched the all-important single goal after just fourteen minutes. The match was best remembered for a brutal tackle

The glitzy eighties set Wembley rocking, this gig being The Rolling Stones in 1982.

Hero of the 1980 Cup Final was Trevor Brooking (*left*), whose header provided West Ham with the only goal of the match. Here he tussles with Liam Brady of Arsenal.

by Arsenal's Willie Young, which, in the last minutes, prevented a second West Ham goal. The victim was Paul Allen – at seventeen years and 256 days, the youngest player to appear in an FA Cup Final.

In 1981, the Rugby League Challenge Cup was contested for the eightieth time – its forty-sixth appearance at Wembley. Widnes, on their fifth visit to the Stadium, beat Hull Kingston Rovers 18–9 to take the trophy home to Lancashire. As a gauge of the sport's popularity, a crowd of more than 92,000 brought in unprecedented gate receipts of almost £600,000.

Women's hockey, which had gone from strength to strength since being introduced to Wembley in 1951, reached its pinnacle in 1981 when the Queen, patron of the All England Women's Hockey Association, attended the match between England and Wales. She toured the ground in an open Royal Range Rover before a dramatic game, which England won 2–1. The scores were level with just four minutes to go when Jan Jurischka replaced Jane Swinnerton for England. She got just one touch of the ball before a Welsh defender brought down Val Robinson, resulting in a penalty stroke. Jurischka, with only her second touch of the game, sank the penalty to give England victory.

That year's English Football League Cup went to Liverpool, who needed a replay to overcome West Ham. The following year, the trophy was renamed the 'Milk Cup' when the Milk Marketing Board began their six-year sponsorship – and the 'Reds' must have got a liking for their 'pintas', because they won the trophy four times in a row until 1984.

The 1981 FA Cup proved particularly memorable with Manchester City starting strongest against Spurs, forcing four corners in the first five minutes. Their pressure paid off after thirty minutes when the oldest man on the park, Tommy Hutchinson, thirty-three, headed home. Spurs, with Argentinians Ossie Ardiles and Ricky Villa in the side, came back to life in the second half when a Glenn Hoddle free kick was deflected past Joe Corrigan in the City goal by Hutchinson – who became only the second player to score for both sides in a Cup Final. (Bert Turner had done the same thing for Charlton Athletic back in 1946.)

Despite extra time, no further goals were scored and the replay five days later was the first to be staged at Wembley. Spurs swiftly took first blood with a strike from Villa in the eighth minute but City's Steve Mackenzie equalised spectacularly three minutes later. A Kevin Reeves penalty put City ahead in the second half but, with eighteen minutes to go, Garth Crooks put Spurs level again. Then, five minutes later, Ricky Villa scored the best goal of his Tottenham career with a sizzling solo run and emphatic finish – which in 2001 would be voted Wembley's goal of the century.

Ricky Villa of Spurs scored the 'Goal of the Century' in the 1981 Cup Final replay with Manchester City.

The year marked Spurs' sixth appearance in an FA Cup Final, of which they had won every one. Incredibly, they did it again the following year and in the same fashion. They fought out a 1–1 draw with Queen's Park Rangers, with Hoddle for Spurs and Terry Fenwick for QPR getting the goals. Again, they lifted the Cup in the replay. Even then, it took a Glenn Hoddle penalty to separate Spurs from the battling Second Division side – managed, incidentally, by Terry Venables, later to become Spurs, then England, boss.

England themselves had struggled through the 1982 World Cup, barely scraping a place in Spain. Once there, they proved uninspired, failing to reach the semi-finals. However, just before Christmas 1982, they appeared at Wembley on the trail of the European Championships, with an emphatic 9–0 win over lowly Luxembourg – a margin of victory not recorded in many internationals. Sadly, it wasn't enough to help England qualify for the finals of this tournament either.

A far greater Wembley crowd-pleaser in 1982 was an overseas visitor who brought unstinting cheer. On 29 May, Pope John Paul II celebrated Mass in front of a capacity 80,000 crowd, while millions more watched on television. Religious terms are often used by the sporting faithful to describe Wembley but this was an occasion when normal superlatives were inadequate. Not too many of those in the crowd realised, but celebrating Mass at Wembley was also a special experience for the Pope himself. While he was a young man in training, he was based for a while in Fulham. A keen football follower, he made several visits to Craven Cottage, and like all football fans, he was keen for an opportunity to visit the mighty Wembley.

Other prayers of the hopeful were voiced the following year, but for an arguably lesser cause. Brighton and Hove Albion lifted themselves from the despair of relegation to force a 2–2 draw in the Cup Final against mighty Manchester United. Their captain, Steve Foster, fought a High Court battle for the right to appear in the final, having been suspended before the big day. Sadly for him, he lost – as did his teammates in the replay. It had seemed as though the whole country was willing Brighton to salvage something from a

Visiting soccer fan Pope John Paul II celebrates Mass before a capacity 80,000 Wembley crowd in 1982.

desperate season. Gordon Smith and Gary Stevens cancelled out strikes from United's Frank Stapleton and Ray Wilkins to earn a replay, but when it was played with Foster back in the team, they were no match for the rampant Reds. England's Bryan Robson led the demolition with two goals as United cruised to a 4–0 victory – the day after Sir Matt Busby's seventy-fourth birthday.

An invasion of American-style hysteria also swept the Stadium in 1983. The Minnesota Vikings and the St Louis Cardinals became the first professional American football teams to take the legendary field of play. It was to herald an exciting future of gridiron at Wembley, as we will see.

Everton ended years of torment and a topsy-turvy season when they lifted the FA Cup in 1984 with a 2–0 win over Watford. It was the end of a long, hard climb from the Fourth Division for Watford — no doubt taking the Yellow Brick Road as their chairman was the effervescent icon of pop, Elton John. He must have enjoyed Wembley so much, despite the 2–0 defeat, that he was back in June to perform a concert in his platform boots and trademark spectacles. Maybe Bob Dylan, who appeared at the Stadium in July, could have dedicated one of his more mournful songs to poor Watford. In any event, Manchester United punished Everton by beating them 1–0 to win the Cup in 1985.

*   *   *   *   *

As we have seen, by this time Wembley was increasingly becoming a venue for pop music megastars, but nothing had prepared the world for 13 July 1985 and the greatest concert ever held. It was titled Live Aid and it united the whole world of music in an unprecedented effort to raise millions of pounds for the millions of people who were starving to death in Africa through failed harvests.

The summer of 1985 will always be remembered for the greatest concert ever seen ... Live Aid.

More than 70,000 fans packed Wembley, but another 1.4 billion watched Live Aid on television across the world.

With a team led by Bob Geldof, lead singer with The Boomtown Rats, the biggest talents of the age – Paul McCartney, Mick Jagger, David Bowie, Madonna, Elton John, Queen and many, many more – happily gave their services free. For the occasion, Wembley was linked by satellite to the John F. Kennedy Stadium in Philadelphia, where another concert was being held in tandem. More than 70,000 people crammed into Wembley itself, but more than 1.4 billion watched worldwide – the biggest TV audience ever recorded.

Status Quo opened the show with the anthem song *Rocking All Over The World*, and from then on, the talent and the tears flowed. Phil Collins had the distinction of appearing on both sides of the Atlantic, flying on Concorde between the two venues. And Queen's twenty-minute set has since been voted the greatest live performance in the history of rock music.

Bob Geldof, the prime moving force behind Live Aid, shakes hands with Roger Daltrey of The Who.

Bernard Doherty, who organised coverage of the event, recalled:

> We had three weeks to get this massive thing off the ground. No rock star could go anywhere without being press-ganged by someone from Live Aid. But unbelievably the whole day went like clockwork. I'll never forget going into David Bowie's dressing room after he'd performed *Heroes* and he just put his face in his hands and cried. It was such an emotional event to be involved with.

With Bob Geldof constantly pleading and swearing at people to give, Live Aid raised more than £70 million for charity. 'I always knew Live Aid would have to be the biggest show ever,' said Geldof. 'After all, it was in aid of an almost biblical disaster.'

*   *   *   *   *

Worthy of less praise than Live Aid was England's build-up to the Mexico World Cup, with a 1–1 draw with Romania in September, balanced by a 5–0 stuffing of Turkey in October. The team went out to the searing heat of Mexico the following summer

107

Liverpool's Craig Johnston leaps for joy after scoring the 1986 Cup Final. Ian Rush (*left*) also scored twice to defeat Everton 3–1.

'Man with a mission': Frank Bruno.

only to return home as beaten quarter-finalists – thanks to the infamous 'Hand of God' goal from Argentina's Diego Maradona, who clearly punched the ball over Peter Shilton but was nevertheless given the goal by Tunisian referee Ali Ben Nasser. As a consolation prize, England ace Gary Lineker won the 'Golden Boot' award as the tournament's top scorer.

A month earlier, the whole of Merseyside had descended on Wembley for the 1986 FA Cup Final as Liverpool took on derby rivals Everton – two teams that were then widely regarded as the English league's leading club sides – the match being played only seven days after Liverpool had secured the League title, with Everton finishing as runners-up. Ian Rush was at the height of his devastating goal-scoring talents for Liverpool, while Gary Lineker played for Everton. Lineker put Everton ahead in the first half but Liverpool went on to win with two goals from Rush and one from Craig Johnston.

On the music scene that summer, Wham's hit-making duo George Michael and Andrew Ridgeley drove the crowds wild, followed by soccer-mad singer Rod Stewart, who staged a concert in July. Queen, enjoying a renaissance since Live Aid, also packed the Stadium that month.

This was also the summer when Britain's boxing hero Frank Bruno got ready to rumble in front of fanatical Wembley supporters. Although ahead on points at the halfway stage against American Tim Witherspoon, big Frank quickly began to run out of steam, while his opponent continued in his languid style. Nevertheless, the fight still seemed relatively close on the cards when the end came. Just three seconds before the bell was due to finish the eleventh round, Bruno was sent reeling from a vicious late assault and the bout was stopped, with Bruno left defenceless and senseless.

Despite losing that bruising battle, Bruno bounced back as a man with a mission. He and Mike Tyson were said to be 'getting it on' for a bone-crushing world title fight at Wembley the following year. But it was the Wembley clash that never was, because the money men couldn't get the deal together. Frank did go on to fight Tyson twice in the States, but lost both times.

*   *   *   *   *

Other American visitors that year left a more lasting legacy. American football, which had been tentatively introduced in 1983, returned in force three years later – and the glamour of gridiron transformed the Stadium into a multi-coloured tapestry.

The US National Football League, which had long been looking to promote American football in other countries, launched a series of exhibition games at Wembley called the American Bowl, involving a number of NFL teams playing pre-season games outside their home country for the first time.

As was befitting the venue of legends, the NFL sent its very best to showcase its product: the Dallas Cowboys and the Chicago Bears. The Cowboys, renowned the world over as 'America's team', and the Bears, reigning Super Bowl champions, had grown their UK fan bases exponentially after British TV had introduced to millions of viewers a sport that most of them barely understood! Chicago's Walter Payton and Jim McMahon were obvious attractions to the Wembley fans but it was the massive figure of their media-hyped teammate William 'The

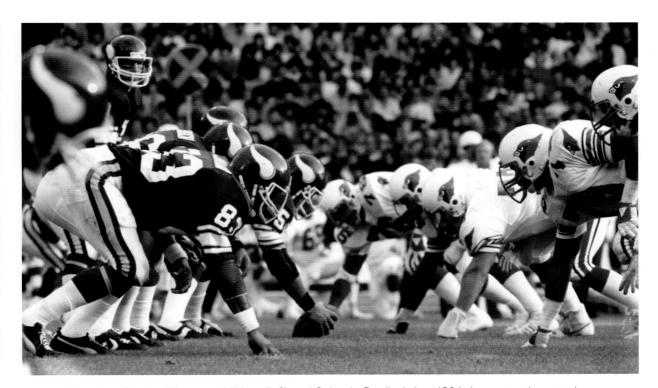

American Bowl ... Minnesota Vikings (*left*) and St Louis Cardinals in a 1986 demonstration match.

NFL brought extra glamour to the Stadium.

Refrigerator' Perry that sent Britain gridiron crazy. With 'The Fridge' in town, the success of the American Bowl seemed assured.

On 3 August, a seam-bursting 82,699 supporters arrived in their favourite NFL team shirts, regardless of whether or not they followed the Bears or Cowboys. The colours on show were badly needed because the game was marked by black skies and heavy rain, but despite soggy field conditions, the carnival never let up. With a 17–6 victory to the Bears, the success of this first officially sanctioned NFL venture into Europe lit the flame to grow American football worldwide. The NFL returned the American Bowl to Wembley for the next seven years, showcasing such great names as Joe Montana with the San Francisco 49ers, Dan Marino of the Miami Dolphins and John Elway of the Denver Broncos. By 1992, NFL business in Europe was turning over $300 million per year, $50 million of that in Britain alone. The experiment of 1986 had paid off.

*   *   *   *   *

Meanwhile, under new chairman Brian Wolfson, Wembley's management was hatching fresh plans to bring the venue up to date and set the scene for new leisure interests. These began to take shape in 1987, when, in a multi-million-pound redevelopment, computerised scoreboards were erected and the Stadium became all-seater, with plush new executive boxes and club suites. Capacity became 80,000, all seated, and 74,000 for concerts.

Pools giants Littlewoods swooped in with sponsorship of the Football League's trophy in 1987, which became the Littlewoods Cup for four years. Old rivals Arsenal and Liverpool competed, the Gunners taking home the Cup after a thrilling 2–1 win.

The FA Cup Final of 1987 also went down as a classic. Pundits said Coventry City's 3–2 win over Spurs showed the world that English football was back to its best. Coventry, the underdogs, came back from the worst possible start, falling behind after just one minute and fifty-two seconds. Spurs drew level 2–2 until, in extra time, they let the Cup slip away when a heartbreaking deflection off Gary Mabbutt meant an own goal – and Coventry carving their name in the record books. There was even more trouble for Spurs because half the team turned out in shirts that did not carry their sponsor's logo. Brewers Holsten had paid £1 million for a three-year contract with Tottenham but no one in the Spurs camp could explain why half a dozen players managed to turn out in shirts that were plain white. 'There were seventeen people in the dressing room other than the players and no one spotted half the team were wearing the wrong shirts,' said one baffled official.

On the music scene there was a growing feeling that Wembley was the only big gig in town. Pop queen Madonna played three hot Stadium dates in the summer of 1987, along with gigs by Bowie, Genesis and U2. Michael Jackson made his Wembley debut the following year, and during five days in July and two in August attracted 504,000 spectators – a record at one venue. His sheer pulling power dwarfed that of pop legends Pink Floyd and even showed Bruce Springsteen who was Boss. The first big non-sporting event of the year had been a tribute to South African leader Nelson Mandela, and a concert in aid of Amnesty International brought things to a close in September.

On the sporting front, lowly Wimbledon humbled mighty Liverpool in the 1988 FA Cup Final with victory from a Lawrie Sanchez header in the thirty-fifth minute. The Wombles turned football upside down and pundits claimed it was 'a custard pie in the face of predictability'.

England, heading for a nightmare in the European Championships, warmed up with a 1–0 win over Scotland and a 1–1 draw with Columbia in a three-way Rous Cup.

The decade drew to a close with Wembley hosting some twenty-four events from March to December 1989, from England versus Belgium at schoolboy level to women's international hockey, a variety of smaller domestic football trophies, the pre-season friendly Makita Tournament and concerts by Cliff Richard, Bros and Simple Minds. Evangelist Billy Graham drew 73,500 to his latest 'mission' and American football drew slightly more to watch Philadelphia beat Cleveland in the American Bowl. Britain's own 'oval ball' game attracted 78,000 as Wigan trounced St Helens in the Rugby League Cup Final.

The Prince of Wales meets the King of Pop (*above*) in 1988, whilst Princess Diana turns up for the same year's Cup Final between Wimbledon and Liverpool.

Princess Diana congratulates giant-killers Wimbledon, who beat Liverpool in the 1988 Cup Final.

In a remarkable FA Cup Final, another all-Merseyside affair saw Liverpool get the better of Everton with a 3–2 win after extra time, with one goal from John Aldridge and two from Ian Rush. Stuart McCall scored both Everton goals, the second being an equaliser just fifteen seconds from the end of normal time. Ian Rush, who had been brought on as a substitute in place of John Aldridge, scored the vital final goal in extra time.

That memorable final was played only five weeks after the Hillsborough disaster, in which ninety-six Liverpool fans had been killed by a crush at Sheffield Wednesday's ground. Before kick-off at Wembley there was a minute's silence and the teams wore black armbands as a sign of respect. Gerry Marsden, lead singer of Mersey band Gerry and the Pacemakers, led the crowd in a rendition of his *You'll Never Walk Alone*, the anthem that had become synonymous with Liverpool Football Club.

*   *   *   *   *

The Stadium that began life expecting to host just two football matches a year was, by the start of the 1990s, massively in demand. In just eight months of 1990, an incredible thirty-six events took place, attracting 2 million visitors through the doors. The FA Cup Final alone brought in 160,000 – because Manchester United and Crystal Palace couldn't settle things at the first attempt, drawing 3–3 after extra time. In the replay,

Crystal Palace's Gary O'Reilly heads past Manchester United goalie Jim Leighton in the 3–3 draw 1990 Cup Final. United won the replay, its first trophy under manager Alex Ferguson.

United won 1–0. Another reason for the busy calendar was that this was the first year promotional play-offs took place at Wembley.

England, with their sights set on Italy and the World Cup Finals, beat Czechoslovakia 4–2 and Denmark 1–0 in friendlies, although they lost 2–1 to Uruguay just three days before they were due to leave.

A glorious run of results in Italy saw them get to the semi-finals, only to lose out to their old sparring partners West Germany in a dramatic penalty shoot-out. Back home, they repaired the hurt with a 2–0 win over Poland in a Euro Championship qualifier.

A roar of approval greeted Great Britain's Rugby League heroes when they walloped Australia in front of an enthralled Wembley crowd in October. Inspired by Ellery Hanley and Paul Schofield, the Brits overturned the Aussies, against the odds, for the first time in eleven years. It was a typically battling performance in front of 52,274 fans, and Great Britain ran out 19–12 victors.

On the music front, The Rolling Stones gathered legions of new fans when they hit Wembley with five tour dates. Just under 200,000 turned out to see them over three days in July, and a further 142,000 came out in August. British audiences were also still mad on Madonna: 220,500 saw her at Wembley over three days just after The Stones' concerts in July.

American football became a regular Wembley feast in 1991 with the creation of a home-grown team, the London Monarchs. NFL bosses in New York had been impressed by the way in which Wembley had staged the American Bowl. Likewise, the British fan

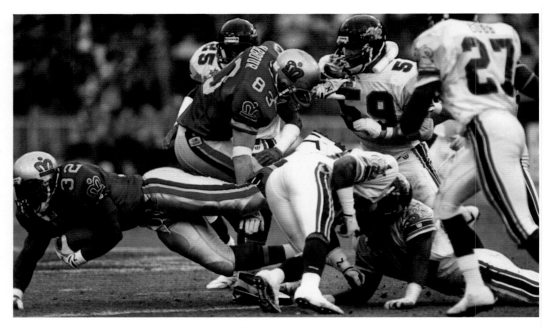

London Monarchs (in blue) reigned in the 1991 World Bowl after crushing Barcelona Dragons 20–0.

base had grown and there was a demand for more of the same. But while the Bowl was a feast of entertainment, it lacked one crucial factor – competition. The sport's leading commentator, journalist Keith Webster, explained:

> The attraction had always been in seeing the biggest names in the game plying their trade. But as these were only NFL pre-season friendlies, those big stars only played for a short while and fans then had to be content with reserve players trying to prove to their coaching staffs that they were worthy of a place in the team when the season started a few weeks later. With this in mind, the World League of American Football was invented and London was named as one of ten franchises, joining Frankfurt, Barcelona, Montreal and six US cities. When it came to deciding on a name for the team, the Monarchs was a runaway choice. As for a venue, there was never any doubt – Wembley was the only place to be.

And so it was that the newly formed London Monarchs regally marched in to win the inaugural World League title. In March 1991, they defeated the New York Knights and a week later they rained on the parade of Orlando Thunder. With regular crowds approaching 50,000, they would suffer only one home defeat out of the ten, the final game at Wembley, when they lost narrowly 17–20 against Barcelona Dragons. The Monarchs then travelled to America and defeated the New York/New Jersey Knights in the play-offs, earning them a berth in the first World Bowl to be played on home territory at Wembley, with a chance to avenge their one defeat against the Dragons. On 9 June, the Stadium was a sea of Union Jacks and Crosses of St George as the Dragons were put to the sword. The score was a resounding 21–0 to the Monarchs, the only team to have beaten Barcelona in the entire season.

As the final gun sounded and the Monarchs players climbed the steps to the Royal Box to receive the inaugural World Bowl trophy, the 60,000-plus crowd broke into a chorus of *We Will Rock You*, the team's unofficial anthem for their championship season. It was a fitting tribute to Wembley, which had rocked all year long to a 'foreign' sport.

The Monarchs returned in 1992 to play again at Wembley but failed to repeat their success on or off the field as the league ran into financial trouble, largely because of disappointing levels of success on the other side of the Atlantic. 'But nothing,' recalled Keith Webster, 'could take away the memories of one glorious season at Wembley, a season where Wembley put the Monarchs, the World League and the sport of American football firmly on the worldwide sporting map.'

While one sport was marking spectacular 'firsts', another was being bid farewell. Sadly, March 1991 marked the last great women's hockey occasion at Wembley. The All England Women's Hockey Association had agreed that an artificial surface offered the best platform and England against France was to be the last international on the famous turf, on which Jane Sixsmith clocked up her fiftieth cap. Disappointingly, England's forty-first encounter at Wembley was won by France, 2–1.

The FA Cup saw a curiosity this year: a semi-final being played on the Wembley turf. Arsenal were drawn against Spurs and Wembley was considered the only viable 'neutral' ground the two North London clubs could feasibly use for such an important game. Spurs triumphed 3–1 in what must have been the only semi-final ever to draw a crowd of 80,000. They faced Brian Clough's Nottingham Forest in the final, which became noted for the bizarre 'death wish' behaviour of their eccentric midfield genius Paul Gascoigne. Even before the kick-off, Gazza was grabbing and kissing Royal hands and attempting to knock the hats off bandsmen as they marched into the centre of the pitch. Within minutes of the start, he had left his stud marks on the first Forest chest he came across and then, fifteen minutes into his first final, he made the strange and irrational challenge that saw

Spurs maverick Paul Gascoigne in agony after a reckless challenge on Nottingham Forest's Gary Charles in the 1991 Cup Final.

Nottingham Forest keeper Mark Crossley dives to save a penalty from Gary Lineker in the 1991 Final.

him carted off to hospital – and out of the game he loved for more than a year. With the teams equal at 1–1 in extra time, Forest defender Des Walker cruelly headed into his own goal to allow Terry Venables to claim the Cup for his Spurs side.

Once again, it was to be a busy year for Wembley throughout 1992, with the London Monarchs now well established, the various soccer finals, league play-offs, Rugby League Challenge Cup, a European Cup Final (Barcelona beat Sampdoria of Italy 1–0 after extra time), the launch of the English Premier League, Rugby Union and League internationals, plus a whole raft of concerts.

In the FA Cup, Liverpool proved too strong for Second Division Sunderland and goals from Michael Thomas and Ian Rush gave them a 2–0 win. It was just what the doctor ordered for Liverpool boss Graeme Souness. He had left hospital just thirty-two days earlier after a triple heart bypass operation.

Top musical attractions that year included Guns 'n' Roses, followed by three dates from Elton John and Eric Clapton appearing together. Then Mick Hucknall's Simply Red, Bryan Adams and six sell-out dates from Michael Jackson brought in record attendances of almost half a million. One of the biggest events of the year was the tribute to Freddie Mercury featuring George Michael, David Bowie, Liza Minelli and the remaining members of Queen.

Even vaster audiences were drawn to Wembley in 1993 when the artist formerly known as Prince filled the Stadium for a one-off concert whilst U2 drew more than 250,000 to a four-night extravaganza in August. Jean Michel Jarre entertained with his electronic wizardry and Madonna returned for another couple of sell-out shows.

In the world of rugby, while Union code sides found it impossible to handle the New Zealand All-Blacks, the Great Britain Rugby League test side put their New Zealand counterparts to the sword with a 17–0 victory.

Incredibly, both FA Cup semi-finals again ended up coming to Wembley in 1993. Sheffield United were drawn against Sheffield Wednesday, and Arsenal faced Spurs for the second time in three years. Whatever happened, it was going to be a Sheffield versus London final and, in the event, it was Wednesday who returned to face Arsenal on 15 May. Arsenal boss George Graham was looking for a unique 'Grand Slam' to become the first man to capture three top trophies as both a player and a manager. His side had already

Cap that! Bruce Grobbelaar celebrates Liverpool's 1992 Cup victory.

earned two League Championships and two League Cup victories in seven years but the FA Cup had eluded him. The game wasn't a classic and ended in a draw after extra time. The replay five days later also went to extra time and was a bruising, bloody battle. Arsenal's giant defender Andy Linighan broke his nose, a finger and Sheffield Wednesday's hearts when he headed the victory goal in the 121st minute.

The England team had been fighting to win 1994 World Cup qualification but, despite a couple of encouraging early results at Wembley, the results didn't come and the most hyped World Cup of modern times would take place without the founding fathers of football.

But the year 1994 was magic for Manchester United. As mentioned, the previous year had seen the launch of the English Premier League, featuring the elite of soccer teams, made up of the twenty-two clubs that had broken away from the Football League at the end of the 1991–92 season. The Premiership season had begun in August, backed by a five-year £305 million deal with BSkyB to televise its matches.

In concept, the Premier League was identical to the old First Division of the Football League, which was now reduced to three divisions. The first Premier League title went to Manchester United – who went on to seal their first League and Cup double with a

4–0 thumping of Chelsea in the FA Cup. Flamboyant Frenchman Eric Cantona scored twice, and Mark Hughes and Brian McClair picked up another couple. Steve Bruce and Gary Pallister were rock solid at the heart of United's defence – and when Chelsea managed to bypass those two 'twin towers', they were stopped by the Great Dane, Peter Schmeichel. It encouraged United chairman Martin Edwards to label his double-winning side their 'greatest ever'.

There was less boasting the following year when Manchester United, still the firm FA Cup favourites, were dethroned when a late goal from Paul Rideout gave Everton a shock 1–0 win. The game's other major piece of silverware in 1995 also ended up on Merseyside as Liverpool beat Bolton Wanderers 2–0 in the Coca Cola Cup.

Other soccer highlights, if they can be described as such, included a visit by Brazil, who produced a bit of spicy Samba magic to beat England 3–1 in June. The visit of Columbia in September resulted in a goalless draw in front of only 20,000 fans. Gates weren't much better as England beat Switzerland 3–1 in November and drew 0–0 with Portugal in December.

There was more drama to delight sports fans, however, when the 'big hitters' arrived – Britain's boxing favourite Frank Bruno and the Rugby League World Cup teams. The bruisers from Down Under tore Great British rugby apart with a 16–8 victory in the RL World Cup Final. The Australians lost to Great Britain in the opening game at Wembley in September but returned just over a month later to exact a hard-fought revenge. In the domestic rugby scene, they didn't come much bigger in 1995 than all-conquering Wigan. A 30–10 victory over Leeds completed a record eight successive Challenge Cup wins, starting back in 1988. The game brought in record receipts as the tally topped £2 million for the first time.

Meanwhile, the other 'big hitter', Britain's oft-battered 'Big Frank' Bruno, strode into the ring on 2 September 1995 and achieved a lifetime's ambition by winning a World Heavyweight title. Such was his immense popularity that Bruno was the only fighter to top the bill twice in the open air of Wembley Stadium. Even the Arena, with its 12,000 capacity, wasn't big enough to accommodate his vast legion of supporters.

Bruno had first challenged for the world title (WBA version) back in the summer of 1986, when he was worn down and stopped in the eleventh round by American Tim Witherspoon. 'But I never gave up dreaming of that title, even after I had been beaten in two more bids, by Mike Tyson and then Lennox Lewis,' he said. Such was the overwhelming national desire to see him succeed that another 30,000-plus crowd were lured to the Stadium to cheer him on against another American, Oliver 'the Atomic Bull' McCall. And after twelve rounds Bruno finally achieved his goal by outpointing McCall to capture the world title the American had plundered from Lennox Lewis a year earlier.

To be blunt, it was an occasion more memorable for the result than the performance. McCall was a pale shadow of the snarling warrior who had previously overwhelmed Lennox Lewis. Bruno, despite having to survive a desperate late assault, was able to hang on for a victory that was perhaps a reward for his perseverance over so many years.

Bruno was later smashed to ignominious defeat by the mighty fists of Mike Tyson in his first defence. But nothing will ever take away the feeling of achievement he enjoyed that autumn night in North London as he proudly strapped on the WBC belt. The normally modest Frank said:

Whatever happens to me now – if I'm shot tomorrow, if I fall under a bus, if I'm run over by a train – nobody can ever take this away from me. I'll be in the record books forever as heavyweight champion of the world. No wonder I love Wembley!

There were also a few 'big hitters' of the music world at the Stadium that year. The ageless Rolling Stones returned to pull in more than 207,000 fans over three summer nights, while Jon Bon Jovi rocked the Stadium with almost 180,000 fans on his three dates. No one, however, could fill a stadium like Rod Stewart. The Tartan Terror opted to play just one Wembley gig and a massive 83,000 screaming fans flocked to see it. Also flying high were The Eagles, Tina Turner, Bryan Adams and The Three Tenors, who all entertained generous Wembley crowds in 1996, whilst Michael Jackson was to return with a real *Thriller* the following year.

Meanwhile, in the 1996 Rugby League Challenge Cup, the sport's unluckiest player was at Wembley again. Paul Loughlin has reached the final four times – and lost in all of them. He got there with St Helens in 1987, 1989 and 1991, and then in April 1996 with Bradford Bulls – when they were beaten by St Helen's! Although the Bulls lost, it was an extra special day for their skipper Robbie Paul, at twenty years and three months, the youngest ever

The Rugby League Challenge Cup Final was dominated by Wigan in the 1990s, winning a record seven in a row from 1989 to 1995. Widnes (white shirts) were the victims in 1993, losing 20–14.

A Wigan tackle during the 1995 Challenge Cup Final when they beat Leeds 30–10.

Wigan's supremacy ended in 1996, when St Helens celebrated a 40–32 victory over Bradford.

Challenge Cup Final captain. Paul, a confident Kiwi who often had to play in the shadow of his elder brother, Wigan star Henry Paul, came of age that day with a performance that many acclaimed as the greatest ever seen from a Wembley debutante. A few days before the game, sponsors Silk Cut had offered £100,000 to the first person to score a hat-trick of tries at Wembley and Paul, despite his side losing 40–32, duly responded. He ran in three superb tries, including one virtuoso display from the halfway line that had the capacity crowd on its feet. This not only earned him a mammoth cheque but he was also named the man of the match in a game that saw record after record being smashed.

As soccer fever swept the country in 1996, Manchester United were back for another tilt at the FA Cup – and a glorious League and Cup double. Eric Cantona was good enough to separate the two 'Red Armies' of Manchester and Liverpool, scoring the game's only goal.

*   *   *   *   *

The summer of 1996 was dominated by one great sporting event: Euro '96. And the unanswered question was: Could Terry Venables' England emulate Alf Ramsey's victory back in '66?

The Wembley opening ceremony on 8 June was an explosion of English pride, with knights in armour and St George slaying a smoke-billowing dragon. Sadly, the game that followed, against Switzerland, did not live up to the fanfare. Alan Shearer gave England the lead before the home team flagged embarrassingly. With only minutes remaining, a dubious

High hopes or hot air? Colourful balloons are released to raise England's spirits for Euro '96.

Wembley welcomed Euro '96 with medieval maidens and St George slaying a smoke-billowing dragon.

Paul Gascoigne helped slay Scotland with a spectacular goal.

penalty decision given against Stuart Pearce for handball allowed Switzerland to equalise – and only a breathtaking save from David Seaman just before the whistle spared England's blushes from being a deeper shade of red.

In the second match, against Scotland, Alan Shearer gave England the lead, followed by the most dramatic sixty seconds of the whole tournament. Scotland were awarded a penalty when Tony Adams was judged to have tripped Gordon Durie. Their captain, Gary McAllister, hammered the ball goalwards but Seaman flung himself instinctively in the right direction and the ball soared away for a corner. A long pass found Paul Gascoigne, who spectacularly volleyed it home, securing a 2–0 win.

The final group game saw both England and Holland needing a point to be sure of reaching the last eight, and England finally delivered what the fans expected, with a 4–1 win – Shearer and Teddy Sheringham each scoring twice. The quarter-finals pitched England against Spain but a stalemated game resulted in a penalty shoot-out. The 4–2 victory had superman Seaman rated the best goalkeeper on the planet.

Then, on 26 June, came the real test. Thirty years after winning the World Cup against West Germany, the home team again faced their most formidable foes. Shearer put England ahead in only three minutes but the cheers soon faded when Stefan Kuntz hammered the equaliser past heroic Seaman. The game remained a magnificent but goalless showpiece through to extra time, despite Darren Anderton hitting the post and Gascoigne twice coming within an ace of scoring.

So it was decided on penalties ... and that's when the nation's collective heart, so recently swelled with pride, was eventually

Alan Shearer and Teddy Sheringham were the men of the match against Holland, both scoring twice.

Left: Ecstasy ... Alan Shearer scores in the first three minutes against Germany. *Right*: Agony ... David Seaman makes a despairing dive as Stefan Kuntz scores an equaliser.

broken. Shearer, David Platt, Stuart Pearce, Gascoigne and Sheringham all scored, as did their German opposite numbers. Then, with the nation holding its breath, Gareth Southgate stepped up – and gave keeper Andreas Köpke a pitifully easy save. It was 'sudden death' as Ardy Moller beat Seaman with Germany's next kick. The dream had come to an abrupt end, culminating in a Wembley final in which Germany defeated the Czech Republic 2–0.

*   *   *   *   *

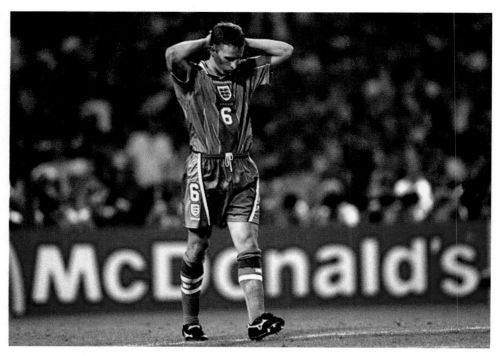

Over and out ... Gareth Southgate is inconsolable after missing the deciding penalty against Germany.

Just a couple of months later, though, it was back to business for the England side as they entertained Poland in yet another crucial World Cup qualifier. Still on a high, England beat the Poles 2–1. Goalkeepers have often thrilled Wembley crowds with wonderful saves or goofy gaffes, but no spectator had ever witnessed a save like the one from Columbia's Higuita on 6 September when England and the South Americans fought out a 0–0 draw. Instead of catching an easy ball, the crazy Columbian threw himself forward, flicked his heels up behind his head, and flipped the ball clear in a gymnastic move he calls his 'Scorpion' save.

The fastest goal ever scored at Wembley was recorded in 1997 by another visitor when Chelsea's Italian international ace Roberto Di Matteo netted after just forty-three seconds as the Blues saw off Middlesbrough 2–0 in the FA Cup. Di Matteo's goal was just two seconds faster than Jackie Milburn's in 1955. Middlesbrough, in the meantime, were on their way to a record and dismally tragic hat-trick. Staring relegation from the Premiership in the face, Bryan Robson's expensive collection of individuals had also battled their way to the Coca Cola Cup Final. Sadly, they also lost that after a Hillsborough replay against Leicester City. On a brighter note, the two teams shared more than £1.75 million from the two games, the final and replay raising around £3.5 million in gate receipts.

The Stadium also saw only its second Rugby Union international, when Wales took on the mighty New Zealand All-Blacks. With their traditional home Cardiff Arms Park closed for renovations, Wembley gave a heroes' welcome to the Welsh but, despite a plucky and fiercely proud display, they were no match for the all-powerful All Blacks.

An optimistic mood greeted World Cup year 1998. After the fabulous displays of Euro '96 and with Glenn Hoddle now at the helm as England manager, fans expected a lot from the national side. The optimism looked slightly misplaced when they lost 2–0 to Chile in a friendly in February and could manage only a goalless draw against Saudi Arabia in May. When they did eventually get to France, a lacklustre start ended in qualification for the knockout stages but, despite a creditable performance, they lost on penalties to old foe Argentina. The French hosts ultimately triumphed, bringing the Jules Rimet Trophy home after sixty years. The bright note for England, however, was the emergence of Liverpool's teenage sensation Michael Owen becoming, at seventeen, the youngest player to win a full England cap

Back at Wembley, the 'Red Army' of Welsh Rugby Union fans returned in March to cheer a magnificent 19–13 Five Nations victory over Scotland. It wasn't to be the start of a Wembley love affair though. In April, the mighty French team were the visitors and Wales got the stuffing knocked out of them, France recording a 51–0 win.

The Coca Cola Cup Final overflowed with drama and emotion on 29 March as Chelsea repeated their 2–0 FA Cup win of the previous season against the same opponents, Middlesborough. It was another heartbreaking final for the Weirsiders but they were comforted by their promotion to the Premiership and the signing of Paul Gascoigne. For Chelsea, both of whose goals were in extra time, it was the chance to reward their player-manager Gianluca Vialli after a difficult season – insisting that Vialli personally receive the trophy, traditionally the role of the winning captain.

When Rugby League fans returned for the Challenge Cup Final in May, a full house of more than 80,000 witnessed one of the game's most spectacular upsets. Sheffield Eagles, the rankest outsiders in the history of their game, were expected to be steamrollered by all-conquering Wigan Warriors. Obviously they hadn't read the script as the Eagles soared to dizzying heights and a 17–8 victory.

The result of the FA Cup Final on that same month was less sensational but still as historic. Arsenal realised a magic double, the greatest dream in English club football, twenty-seven years after they first achieved this remarkable feat. Having clinched the Premier League with a season of outstanding displays, they were just too powerful for Newcastle United. Goals from Dutchman Marc Overmars and French striker Nicolas Anelka made the team's manager, Frenchman Arsene Wenger, the first foreign coach to lift the English double.

Among musical maestros to pack the Stadium, Elton John entertained more than 80,000 fans over two nights in June, followed by the Bee Gees and the Spice Girls as the year drew to a close.

For Wembley itself, three-quarters of a century of history was drawing to a close. The Venue of Legends was due to shut its doors for the last time in 1999 at the conclusion of a magnificent millennium. But its final sporting dramas were still to be played out ...

The Football League Cup Final in March provided Tottenham Hotspur with their third win of the trophy. Spurs won against Leicester City with a last-minute injury time header from Allan Nielsen. Unfortunately, the match was notable for accusations of bad sportsmanship. Tottenham's Justin Edinburgh became the last ever player to be sent off at the old Wembley after supposedly throwing a punch at Leicester's Robbie Savage after a confrontation between the two. But after a post-match analysis, some commentators reported that Savage had overreacted to a minimal contact and that the red card against Edinburgh had been unjustly awarded.

To illustrate the popular strength of Rugby League, more than 73,000 fans turned up in May to see the Leeds Rhinos beat London Broncos 52–16.

The prestige of the two teams that contested the FA Cup Final that month could not have been more different. Manchester United went into the match as champions of England, having clinched the Premier League title in their final game the previous weekend after losing just three league games all season. Unbeaten in their previous thirty-one matches in all competitions, they had also qualified for the 1999 UEFA Champions League Final against Bayern Munich due to be played four days later. By contrast, their opponents, Newcastle United, had finished thirteenth out of the twenty teams in the Premier League and had been knocked out of both the Cup Winners Cup and the League Cup.

The FA Cup drama came in the first eight minutes. Teddy Sheringham replaced an injured Roy Keane and, just ninety seconds after striding onto the pitch, the substitute drifted into the box and, thanks to a pass by Paul Scholes, slotted a low drive past Newcastle goalkeeper Steve Harper. In the second half, Sheringham returned the favour – and the ball – to Paul Scholes, allowing Alex Ferguson's team the luxury of being able to play some exhibition football. United's 2–0 victory meant their tenth FA Cup triumph, a record in English football, as well as securing their third league and cup double in the 1990s.

Scholes was not the flavour of the month when he returned with the England team in June for a Euro 2000 qualifier against Sweden that ended in a goalless draw. Scholes was sent off early in the second half for his second bookable offence and his third bad challenge after, according to one commentator, 'getting away with a horror tackle in the first minute of the game'. The three tackles were in contrast to his hat-trick heroism in a previous Wembley qualifier against Poland in March. The 0–0 score against Sweden ruined England's chances of automatic qualification, compounded by a dismal 0–1 loss to Scotland in November. Nevertheless, the home team succeed on aggregate – only to be eliminated in Belgium the following June.

Before the start of the June match between England and Sweden, a minute's silence had been held following the death of 1966 World Cup winner Sir Alf Ramsey. Although it was less than immaculately observed, it could well have been a moment to reflect on the pending passing of another sporting colossus: Wembley itself. For it had already been announced that the Stadium was to get a red card and be replaced with a fresher substitute.

*   *   *   *   *

It was uncertain at that stage whether a single match would be played on the hallowed turf after the close of the 1999 season. But as debate raged about the design of the new building – and the survival of the Twin Towers in any form – Wembley did witness a few more events.

The Final Whistle ... and it was a damp squib as England fans braved the rain on 7 October 2000 for the last match on Wembley's old turf – a 2002 World Cup qualifier, which Germany won 1–0.

On 20 May 2000, the last FA Cup Final to be played at the old venue saw Chelsea defeat Aston Villa 1–0, with the only goal being scored by Robert Di Matteo. The last competitive club match was the 2000 First Division play-off final on 29 May between Ipswich Town and Barnsley, a 4–2 win for the former resulting in promotion to the Premier League. The last club match was the 2000 Charity Shield on 3 August, when Chelsea beat Manchester United 2–0.

The very last match to be played at the old Wembley Stadium was England versus Germany on 7 October 2000 – a qualifying game for the 2002 World Cup, which also marked Kevin Keegan's retirement as England manager. On that day, Tony Adams made his sixtieth Wembley appearance, a record for any player. Adams had also claimed England's final goal at the Stadium, having scored in the previous home fixture against Ukraine in May. Germany won the game 1–0, with Dietmar Hamann scoring the very last goal on Wembley's old turf.

*   *   *   *   *

127

Even after the final rubber-stamping of the decision to rebuild Wembley, it took more than two years before demolition began, in December 2002. Numerous complications — financial, political and aesthetic — delayed the process, amid doubts from experts and the media that the rebuild would be successful. And in many respects, it had been a highly risky decision. The ground had been in use for more than seventy-five years and was seen by many as one of the greatest stadiums on the planet. Wembley was a Grade II Listed Building and every aspect of its redevelopment would be monitored by English Heritage.

The future of the Twin Towers became an issue of national importance. For many, the iconic 126-foot high structures represented the historical, cultural and international standing of English sport. In practice, they might be little more than glorified stairwells but, as symbols of national identity, to see them go seemed unthinkable. Yet that was indeed their fate and the demolition teams began tearing them down in early 2003. The FA announced during the period just before demolition started that collectors would be able to buy memorabilia from the rubble of the old towers. Whether in the form of salt and pepper grinders or miniature models of the towers themselves, this seemed no more than a minor sop from

A Stadium of Light? This was an early vision for the New Wembley, incorporating the Twin Towers.

The New Wembley ... Gone are the Twin Towers; instead, a soaring arch adorns the London skyline.

the Football Association. However, such souvenir sales would cover only £1 million of the cost, with the FA still needing roughly another £800 million to build the new ground! And when the Australian construction company Multiplex finally handed over the keys to the FA on 9 March 2007, the total cost (including the builder's losses) was reported to have approached £1 billion. But what they got was something pretty spectacular ...

Rising almost 100 metres higher than the beloved Twin Towers it replaced, architect Sir Norman Foster's soaring Wembley Arch was a dramatic decoration to the London skyline. At 315 metres, the Arch is the longest single span roof structure in the world, and lit up at night, is visible right across London. It is set at a jaunty 68-degree tilt from the horizontal and designed to support the 5,000 tonnes of the roof. With a diameter of 7.4 metres, it is wide enough for a Channel Tunnel train to run within it and ensures that, with no need for pillars, the fans' views of the pitch remain unobstructed. The roof, rising 52 metres above the pitch, measures 11 acres, of which four are retractable. The sliding north and south roof sections allow the pitch to be exposed to direct sunlight and ventilation whilst the spectators remain covered.

The bowl-shaped arena beneath it, with a circumference of 1 kilometre, encloses 4 million cubic metres, the equivalent to 25,000 double decker London buses. It allows seating for 90,000 people spread over three tiers in seats that are now higher and closer to the pitch, with substantially more leg room. The Royal Box retains its same position, in the middle of the North Stand – and now has 107 steps up to its presentation platform instead of the thirty-nine of old.

The pitch is also revolutionary. With specially designed protective panels, it was designed to be transformed into an elevated track and athletic arena or a space for large musical events. The first occasion that a ball was kicked on the new turf was a private affair, the pitch being christened with a game played behind closed doors between the staffs of Multiplex and Wembley Stadium.

The first match involving professional players was in March 2007 between England's and Italy's Under-21 sides. In May, the first FA Cup Final, between Manchester United and Chelsea, was a real cliffhanger. It ran into extra time before Didier Drogba made the record books as the first finalist to score, the single goal of the game giving Chelsea their fourth FA Cup.

One of the problems during the reconstruction of the Stadium had been the disruption caused to the England team, who had been forced to travel around the country to play their home games at stadiums such as Old Trafford and Anfield. Although this was great for fans far from London, it did cause disruption for the teams themselves. England had to wait until June 2007 before returning to Wembley. The first game involving a full national side was a friendly against Brazil in which captain John Terry became the Stadium's first England international goal scorer. (Brazil's Diego Ribas da Cunha became the first full international player to score, hence the resulting 1–1 draw.)

There was one other vital element of the Stadium that caused concern: the very grass that was being played on. In its first few years, the pitch had to be relaid ten times. Criticism of the surface – voiced by, among other luminaries, Alex Ferguson, Arsene Wenger, Harry Redknapp and David Moyes – continued through to the 2010 FA Cup Final when, despite beating Portsmouth 1–0, Chelsea captain John Terry complained: 'The pitch ruined the final. It's probably the worst pitch we've played on all year. It's not good enough for Wembley.' Thereafter, the turf was again torn up. This time it was relaid with a successful semi-artificial system known as Desso, a synthetic thread woven into the turf.

Despite these problems, the new Stadium has much to boast about. Apart from being 'the Cathedral of Football', as the legendary Pele described it, Wembley has gone on to create many magical moments, from UEFA Champions League Finals to the return of American football and of Rugby League to dozens of sell-out musical concerts. And its facilities are undoubtedly superior to those in the old building. For instance, the new Stadium has: 164 turnstiles, 380 floodlights, 2 giant TV screens the size of 600 regular tellies, 26 elevators, 98 kitchens serving 10,000 meals, 8 restaurants, 4 banqueting halls, 688 food and beverage service points dispensing 30,000 cups of coffee in ten minutes, the ability to serve 40,000 pints of beer during half-time and, oh yes, 2,618 toilets – supposedly more than any other venue in the world!

Is it lacking anything at all? If the question was raised by a nostalgic fan, the answer might be: 'Just two things.' They are, of course, those massive, magical, world-famous Twin Towers that looked down on so many decades of sporting glory.

It is also astonishing to think that all the Wembley wonders of the last century – Stanley Matthews' fifties footwork, Billy Wright's 100 caps, Henry Cooper's flooring of Clay, England's 1966 World Cup glory, and Live Aid – might never have taken place but for some fast dogs and a white horse called Billy!

Dates and Events

1923	Empire Stadium completed. First FA Cup Final, 28 April: Bolton 2 v 0 West Ham.
1924	King George V opens British Empire Exhibition, 23 April, runs for six weeks.
1925	Empire Exhibition reopens May–Oct then closes with huge financial loss. Rugby Union debut.
1927	New owner Arthur Elvin introduces greyhound racing, drawing crowds of 50,000.
1928	Radio days begin. Inaugural meeting of National Greyhound Racing Society.
1929	Speedway thrills. First Rugby League Cup Final. Mick the Miller wins Greyhound Derby.
1930	*Graf Zeppelin* sails silently overhead.
1934	First baseball – by crew of US warship.
1935	Boxing: Jack Petersen loses to Walter Neusel.
1939	War declared 3 Sept. World Speedway Championships cancelled. Greyhounds evacuated.
1940	Stadium used for Dunkirk evacuees.
1942	Servicemen in amateur Cup Final.
1943	Baseball between US air and ground forces.
1944	German 'doodlebug' lands near kennels; greyhounds scamper. Stanley Matthews reveals his magic.
1945	Victory in Europe thanksgiving service.
1946	Post-war sports attract 4,400,000 fans. Speedway returns: Wembley Lions become National League champs. Rugby League Cup Finals return. Official FA Cup Finals restart.
1947	First photo finish equipment, for greyhounds.
1948	Olympic Games open 29 July. Olympic Way specially constructed.
1950	Capacity increased to 100,000. American football first played.
1951	Jolly hockey sticks for England ladies!
1953	The 'Stanley Matthews Cup Final'. England lose on home soil for first time to a foreign side, Hungary.
1955	Evangelist Billy Graham fills Stadium.
1956	Bert Trautmann's heroism.
1957	Floodlights allow mid-week evening games. Speedway suspended. Arthur Elvin dies.
1958	Tragedy strikes Manchester United but they still make it to the Cup Final.
1959	Billy Wright's 100th cap. Broken leg brings call for substitutes.

1961	It's snow joke: ski jumping comes to Wembley.
1963	Henry Cooper floors Cassius Clay.
1966	World Cup wonder.
1967	Football League Cup arrives.
1968	Royal International Horse Show at the Stadium – soon banished to Wembley Arena after damaging the treasured turf.
1972	German revenge for World Cup defeat. Rock 'n' Roll years begin, with Bill Haley & co.
1974	Bill Shankly's 'Red Army' storm in.
1975	Second Division underdogs Southampton beat top dogs Man United.
1981	Wembley hosts 100th FA Cup Final and 80th Rugby League Challenge Cup.
1982	Pope John Paul II celebrates Mass.
1984	Elton John plays Wembley – and so does his team.
1985	Live Aid rocks the world.
1986	NFL's American Bowl launched.
1987	Redevelopment introduces all-seating and computerised scoreboards.
1988	Michael Jackson attracts record half-million fans.
1989	England's 100th match at Wembley.

1990	Two million visitors attracted to thirty-six events.
1991	Monarchs win first American Football World League. Hockey ladies take their leave.
1992	Premier League launched.
1995	Big Frank Bruno is champ.
1996	Football comes home for Euro '96
1999	Wembley Stadium due to close.
2000	The very final FA Cup Final. German scores last goal on Wembley's old turf.
2001	Storm over plans to demolish Twin Towers.
2003	Wembley Stadium finally demolished.
2007	New Wembley Stadium opens.